The Five

Sarah Bartlett is a profe... astrology columns f... Cosmopolitan magazine. ...author of many books including the bestselling *Feng Shui for Lovers*. She lives in Saffron Walden.

Also by Sarah Bartlett

Feng Shui for Lovers

SARAH BARTLETT

The Five Keys of
Feng Shui

ORION

An Orion paperback

First published in Great Britain in 1998
by Vista, an imprint of the Cassell Group
This paperback edition published in 2001
by Orion Books Ltd,
Orion House, 5 Upper St Martin's Lane,
London WC2H 9EA

A CIP catalogue record for this
book is available from the British Library.

ISBN 0 57540 329 2

Printed and bound in Great Britain by
The Guernsey Press Co. Ltd, Guernsey, C.I.

To my father, F.D.R.

Contents

Introduction

Feng Shui is about more than just moving your furniture, changing your interior decor and decluttering your home. It is also about the art of harmonious living. The word Feng means 'Wind' and Shui means 'Water', and the ancient Chinese believed that by balancing these two forces of nature they could create harmony in their lives.

The Five Keys of Feng Shui and the art of living a successful lifestyle revolve around the five elements of ancient Chinese astrology. These are quite simply five different types of energy that make up the 'Feng' and the 'Shui' of our environment and that are symbolized by the elements of Metal, Water, Wood, Fire and Earth.

The ancient Chinese mystics believed that everything in the universe was composed of these five energies and their eternal cycle of interaction. The heavens were divided into five palaces where the elements ruled. One palace – the Palace of Earth – became

FIRE
South

WOOD   EARTH   METAL
East   Core   West

WATER
North

Diagram 1
The elements and the compass points

the pivotal point, our world. This world was surrounded by the other four palaces at the points of the
compass – the Palace of Metal in the west, the Palace
of Water in the north, the Palace of Wood in the east
and the Palace of Fire in the south (see Diagram 1).

The five elemental energies are reflected and
expressed in everything, from the natural rhythms of
the world, the solar system, our landscapes, human
bodies, personalities and lifestyle, even our homes and
interiors. Because the home is the most important
location and environment for a person's well-being, it

has always been easier to put Feng Shui principles into practice here.

Resonance

But Feng Shui is also about balancing these elemental energies in other aspects of your lifestyle as well as in your home, to help you lead an enriched and rewarding existence.

Knowing which elemental energy you resonate with at any given time can help to bring harmony to your career, your relationships, your family life, your body and the inner You. Remember how sometimes when you listen to music a certain chord almost touches your soul? This is when you are in harmony with a particular musical note, and it exactly mirrors the kind of resonance we experience with the invisible energies of the elements.

The five elements not only reflect our inner qualities and the way we express ourselves but are also mirrored and balanced by the world outside us. Our friends, partners, work, family, spiritual path, relationships, ambitions, world vision, creative abilities, values, needs, perception, gardens, homes, fitness, humour, food, desires and many other facets of our lives are influenced by these five key elemental energies. Each one will influence you at some time in your life. This book will show you which element you were born under and which element is primarily influencing you at the moment. By drawing on the secret wisdom of the five elements in Feng Shui, you can complement, enhance and balance the inner you with the outer world.

How to use this book

What are the five elemental palaces?

The palace is the home of each elemental energy. Depending on which element you feel most affinity with, it is behind the palace gates that you can discover how to energize and vitalize your life at any given time. This book is a journey. You may visit all the five palaces at some point in your life, enjoying yourself in any or all of them.

Each palace has a kitchen garden where you will find the ingredients for harmonizing your body, family life and well-being. It is filled with plants, crystals and talismans for outer beauty; creative rituals and chakra work for inner beauty; and ideas for self-pleasure and sweetening your dreams.

Try to work with the energies and qualities in one palace at a time. For each element, you'll find that there are auspicious and inauspicious times of the year for performing certain affirmations, meditations, divinations and rituals and for working with your body or your spiritual development and the placement of Feng Shui cures. Take it slowly. Follow the natural rhythms and cycles of the moon and the sun. Let the energy flow through you rather than you trying to regulate it.

You may find that one elemental palace seems to dominate for a month, or maybe two months, after which a different palace becomes more important and you take a different journey. Wherever you find yourself, enjoy the rituals, the cycles, the balancers, the charms, the remedies and the pathways as you work your way towards a better understanding of the inner elemental you.

What are Yin and Yang?

Yin and Yang are the two balancing forces that make up our world as we know it. In our perception of the world we cannot have light without dark, male without female, up without down, or positive without negative. The continuous interaction of these two opposite energies creates the cosmic pattern of the five elements, from which all objects, feelings and thoughts are created.

When you look up your birth element on pages 20–21, you will see that you were born in either a Yin or a Yang year. This determines your mode of expression. If you were born under a Yin year, you are more inclined towards expressing Yin energy. This is passive, receptive and flowing. If you were born under a Yang year, you are more likely to express Yang energy. This is active, dynamic and potent.

The elemental cycles

Diagrams 2 and 3 show the interaction of the elements. Diagram 2 explains how each element is energized by another and completes a cycle of empowerment. Thus, Wood enflames Fire; Fire nourishes Earth; Earth holds Metal; Metal melts into Water; Water feeds Wood. So, for example, if your birth element is Wood, there is a strong likelihood that you will be vitalized by the elements of Water and Fire in your lifestyle. You may find that Water and Fire people often appear in your life and although you might feel a natural affinity with other

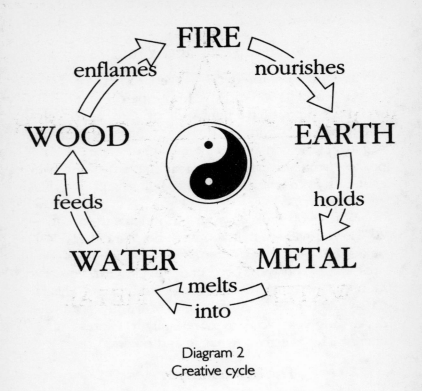

Diagram 2
Creative cycle

Wood people, or for doing Wood things, you may need these other beneficial elements to provide energy and balance.

The second cycle of elemental energy describes how one element can disempower another (see Diagram 3). Thus, Water puts out Fire; Fire melts Metal; Metal chops Wood; Wood draws on Earth; Earth soaks up Water. So, for example, if your birth element is Fire, you may find that Water people make you feel

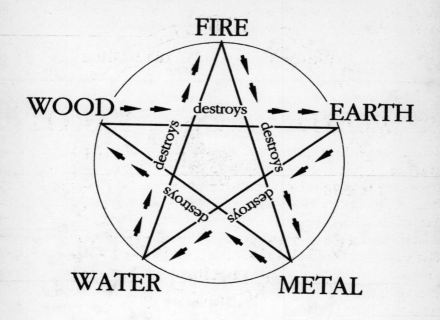

Diagram 3
Destructive cycle

uncomfortable, as if they are draining away your energy or putting a damper on your plans. Although Metal people prove less difficult, you may want to provoke them into action!

The later chapters on the specific elements will also provide an insight into finding inner peace, and indicate who you might find yourself in conflict with and how to avoid scenes.

15

The five elemental palaces

Diagram 4 explains the interaction and traditional associations of the five elemental palaces.

Diagram 4
The traditional associations of the five elemental palaces

Wood: the Green Palace of the Dragon

The Wood Palace resonates to the east, to spring, the colour green and the dragon. This palace is guarded by the Dragon Star, Jupiter.

Fire: the Red Palace of the Phoenix

The Fire Palace resonates to the south, to summer, the colour red and the phoenix. This palace is guarded by the Phoenix Star, Mars.

Earth: the Yellow Palace of the Emperor

The Earth Palace resonates to the centre, to late summer, the colour yellow and the emperor. This palace is guarded by the Emperor Star, Saturn.

Metal: the White Palace of the Tiger

The Metal Palace resonates to the west, to autumn, the colour white and the tiger. This palace is guarded by the Tiger Star, Venus.

Water: the Black Palace of the Tortoise

The Water Palace resonates to the north, to winter, the colour black and the tortoise. This palace is guarded by the Tortoise Star, Mercury.

How to start

First, find out about your own birth element in Chapter 1, to establish the characteristics, qualities and energy style with which you *unconsciously* resonate. But remember, it may be that another element is currently exerting more influence in your life than your birth element. So, first read through your birth element qualities and characteristics to see if you feel comfortable with this energy. If you do not, use the element test in Chapter 2 to establish which element is currently most influential and work with this instead. Keep your birth element in mind. If you find you don't have a current dominant element – perhaps they all have an equal scoring in the Test – then stick to your key birth element.

If you do identify with an element other than your birth element, use the treasures in this elemental palace for outer and inner harmony. If, however, you find that two elements are equally dominant, then work with both in tandem. If you find all the elements are equally balanced in the scoring, then follow your birth element. You can weave in and out of all five elements if and when your energy affinity changes. Harmony is about balancing, integrating and reinforcing all the elements.

Chapter One

You're in Your Element

Table of birth elements

The table of elements, with their corresponding lunar years, for the twentieth century and whether they are Yin or Yang is given on pages 20–21.

The element itself rules for approximately two years and a complete cycle of elements takes ten years; but the change-over days vary considerably from year to year, as you will see.

If you were born either on the very last day of an elemental cycle or the very first day of a new one, it might be advisable to look at both element characteristics, as the actual times of the lunar cycle changes aren't given. You may feel more 'in tune' with one element than the other.

Table 1: Element years

Metal Yang	Water Yang	Wood Yang
31.1.00–18.1.01	8.2.02–28.1.03	16.2.04–3.2.05
10.2.10–29.1.11	18.2.12–5.2.13	26.1.14–13.2.15
20.2.20–7.2.21	28.1.22–15.2.23	5.2.24–24.1.25
30.1.30–16.2.31	6.2.32–25.1.33	14.2.34–3.2.35
8.2.40–26.1.41	15.2.42–4.2.43	25.1.44–13.2.45
17.2.50–5.2.51	27.1.52–13.2.53	3.2.54–23.1.55
28.1.60–14.2.61	5.2.62–24.1.63	13.2.64–1.2.65
6.2.70–26.1.71	16.1.72–2.2.73	23.1.74–10.2.75
16.2.80–4.2.81	25.1.82–12.2.83	2.2.84–19.2.85
27.1.90–14.1.91	4.1.92–22.1.93	10.2.94–30.1.95

Metal Yin	Water Yin	Wood Yin
19.1.01–7.2.02	29.1.03–15.2.04	4.2.05–24.1.06
30.1.11–17.2.12	6.2.13–25.1.14	14.2.15–2.2.16
8.2.21–27.1.22	16.2.23–4.2.24	25.1.25–12.2.26
17.2.31–5.2.32	26.1.33–13.2.34	4.2.35–23.1.36
⊙27.1.41–14.2.42	5.2.43–24.1.44	14.2.45–1.2.46
6.2.51–26.1.52	14.2.53–2.2.54	24.1.55–11.2.56
15.2.61–4.2.62	25.1.63–12.2.64	2.2.65–20.1.66
27.1.71–15.1.72	3.2.73–22.1.74	11.2.75–30.1.76
5.2.81–24.1.82	13.2.83–1.2.84	20.2.85–8.2.86
15.2.91–3.2.92	23.1.93–9.2.94	31.1.95–18.2.96

Now you know which Birth Element you are, turn to the relevant section in this chapter and check its characteristics, expression and qualities before referring to the element test in Chapter 2. Remember that, like any description of 'types', these are model element characters and as such are extreme examples. Sun-sign types

Fire Yang	Earth Yang
25.1.06–12.2.07	2.2.08–21.1.09
3.2.16–22.1.17	11.2.18–31.1.19
13.2.26–1.2.27	23.1.28–9.2.29
24.1.36–10.2.37	31.1.38–18.2.39
2.2.46–21.1.47	10.2.48–28.1.49
12.2.56–30.1.57	18.2.58–7.2.59
21.1.66–8.2.67	30.1.68–16.2.69
31.1.76–17.2.77	7.2.78–27.1.79
9.2.86–28.1.87	17.2.88–5.2.89
19.2.96–7.2.97	28.1.98–5.2.99

Fire Yin	Earth Yin
13.2.07–1.2.08	22.1.09–9.2.10
23.1.17–10.2.18	1.2.19–19.2.20
2.2.27–22.1.28	10.2.29–29.1.30
11.2.37–30.1.38	19.2.39–7.2.40
22.1.47–9.2.48	29.1.49–16.2.50
31.1.57–17.2.58	8.2.59–27.1.60
9.2.67–29.1.68	17.2.69–5.2.70
18.2.77–6.2.78	28.1.79–15.2.80
29.1.87–16.2.88	6.2.89–26.1.90
8.2.97–27.1.98	6.2.99–27.1.2000

are extreme. However, they do carry your essence and the flavour of your energy expression. We are each made up of all the elements, but your birth element should give some insightful clues to your core energy profile.

The element of Wood

Your inner energy is altruistic and poised

Wood in the environment

In traditional Feng Shui Wood is associated with the colour green, the dragon, the east and spring.

Wood is all around us: we make furniture from it and bring plants and shrubs into the gardens we cultivate. The tree has figured in many early civilizations not only as a symbol of growth and fertility but also as a symbol of creativity. Although it takes many years for a tree to grow, the strength and energy required to produce such solidity in a tree trunk have been nourished by Water, its natural ally in the elemental cycle.

Trees also symbolize the rise of our consciousness towards a spiritual goal. Trees take us up above ground level, they make us look to the skies and remember that there is more in heaven and earth than our own perception of reality. Even though we are also rooted to the earth, we can still ascend to the sky through our visions or our beliefs. This is highly reflective of Wood people, who are practical idealists.

A Wood's eye view

Above all I need to maintain my freedom. Although you'll find me surrounded by many acquaintances, there are times when I really prefer to be alone. Sometimes I'd rather be out in the middle of the countryside enjoying the landscape or communing with nature than living a fast-paced existence in the city. However, I'm lucky, because I also feel comfortable in large crowds, where I can maintain my anonymity, sure that no one knows who I am! Space is important to me, whether in my surroundings or with people. If others don't respect this big territory I inhabit, then they can find I'll run a mile to find some more.

I don't actually have many close friends – too much intimacy ties me down, makes me feel uncomfortable. I dislike being committed to other people's personal problems; I'd rather be involved in the bigger issues in life. However, I go overboard sometimes to help people out if they've got issues to resolve, as long as they don't want to cry on my shoulder. That's when I get a sense of claustrophobia, and the feeling I'm going to be stuck with too much emotional contact in my life. Some people call me aloof, even glamorous, but this is because I keep a detached outlook on the world, making sure that no one can see the softer 'me' beneath that cool exterior. Yes, I do have feelings, quite strong ones, but I don't want my vulnerable side to be exposed: there are too many people in the world who would try to take advantage if you let them. So I often get accused of being tough-skinned, when in fact I only want people to be fair. That's why I'm excellent at planning big schemes and getting involved in humanitarian issues and diplomatic affairs, which I find far more challenging than the simple necessities of everyday life. I'm often told I'm quite mysterious and I certainly need to feel special. That's why I have to find myself a niche where I stand out from others. Not necessarily fame and glory; those things are for more ambitious souls. I prefer to stay incognito, and just receive recognition from my peers and colleagues for what I have to offer.

My aesthetic sense is highly developed, and so I enjoy beauty and harmony in my home and at work. But this is more about the beauty of the mind than actual objects. I like to plan first, imagining the strategy required to create something beautiful. My own home must be casual and easy to live in. Definitely not cluttered! But neither must it be so tidy that you can't leave a plate on the table, or a waste-paper basket that hasn't been emptied for a day! I need room to spread out, and although I don't have many possessions, light, space and easy-living are essential requirements.

Quick to respond to ideas, I give as much practical advice as I can think of, especially when someone else has ideals and visions that they can't get off the ground. In business, and in all aspects of work, I can be a useful adviser and strategist. But I prefer to be an organizer and a cooperator rather than a leader or a high-profile, up-front person. Getting dressed up in tailored suits and immaculately cut clothes is OK for a while, if the job dictates it, but on the whole I'd rather be free to wear what I like, when I like. If I'm not out in the big wide world, or travelling as often as I can, I would prefer to do things my own way and work for myself. I'm a perfectionist, but not so much the type who has to put everything in square boxes – more someone who is just very self-possessed and doesn't like to see the flaws in other people's lives. Yes, that makes me sound conceited, and I suppose egotistic, but it's only a reflection of my idealistic view of human nature, that I want everyone else to live up to the high expectations I have for myself.

Being unpossessive I avoid getting involved in too many family or work commitments, and all those social events I'm expected to attend! My many friends often call me weird, and maybe even eccentric. Being described as odd and a bit of a rogue gives me a sense of identity that I find amusing. This is the kind of compliment I enjoy. It marks me out as different. And when people suggest I might even be a bit of a rebel, then I am really roused into action. However, I can become obsessed with being different just for the sake of it, which often makes me quite cantankerous and awkward.

But in my work or career, I aim for harmony for all, and like to contribute to the greater good of the company, the vision or the larger global collective of responsibility. In that way I can avoid having to confront my own deeper needs. Thinking about myself seems unimportant; I'd rather change the world around me. I'm not very good at accepting change in my own life, or my style. I'll often keep the same hairstyle, style of clothes and music, but love to see everyone else respond to the way fashion keeps changing. I can be a great innovator of style, as long as it's for others, and not for myself! Although I am quite proud of my unusual needs, shocking my family or friends with crazy schemes that I rarely put into action is sometimes just a way of asserting my own sense of detachment.

I really believe in the right of the individual, and will fight causes for anyone, as long as they believe in themselves. My own individuality is unique, so I respect that in others. I am notorious for trying to be different just to get noticed. That's my way of getting attention. My main objective in life is to keep things in focus, to be sure about where I am going and not to be too impulsive. I am a skilled diplomat, whether in a working environment or on the home front.

Cooperation is essential. If others trust me – and they usually do – I'll help them out and inspire their confidence. I can provide invaluable emotional and spiritual support, as long as people don't expect too much. Because I'm not overly emotional myself, I can analyse and objectify everyone else's problems, without getting too het up about my own.

Problems are things I don't often have myself, because I try to make sure life is a fairly intellectual process rather than one fraught with feelings. Maybe this makes me seem insensitive, and too concerned with humanitarian issues rather than those of my friends. But getting intimate means I can't spread myself on a grand scale. Intimacy means commitment, and I'd rather be involved in great schemes and large-scale social events than be beholden to any one person.

I spend most of my time looking into the future to see what needs to be done next. Although I'm not particularly intuitive (I mean I'm not particularly clairvoyant), just planning the future and organizing long-term objectives are my joy. My way of playing and experimenting with ideas is to see them bear fruit, to become reality, rather than just vague and insubstantial dreams. Looking back on the past, living in memories and sentimental recollection isn't for me. Science fiction and new technology is more likely to inspire me than a nostalgic film or a book of old photographs retrieved from the family attic.

Desperate to retain my independence, I'm quite hard to handle when it comes to relationships. But in a highly sophisticated way, I love playing the game of seduction. I can be quite alluring, and usually get what I want! Because I'm so sure about myself, I often throw people off balance. I am refined about clothes and my surroundings, and if my partner or friend doesn't share my taste, then I'll soon leave in search of the wide-open spaces! Unusual people turn me on: the more weird they are, the more fascinated I'll be. I tend to analyse them, picking out their qualities and faults and examining them like a Frankenstein experiment until I am sure of their integrity. The only problem is that if they don't live up to my own rather lofty vision of a relationship, then I can become ambivalent and pretty opinionated!

My ideal relationship would have to be something very unconventional. Perhaps a reliable and constant companion, a good friendship with sex thrown in, where we continued to live in different homes? Living with another person would cramp my style and disturb my sense of altruism. Essentially a mental person, I tend to rationalize everything rather than listen to my feelings. So I may sometimes let my partner or companion down or kill off the relationship with too much compliance!

With loads of energy to give to any job, I can usually manage to get more done in a day than most people. I really like to play, whether it's sport, intellectual word games or throwing wild parties. I like to be noticed at parties, and the more outrageous I am the better. Then I can really shine. The more I shine and the more bizarre people think me, the safer I feel. It stops them getting too close to that vulnerable part inside.

My family is important to me, but I believe in the global family rather than the separate suburban unit. This is where I would like things to change. Plans for the world may seem like dreams to many, but this is my vision for the future: to improve life, to ensure peace and happiness for every living thing. An impossible dream perhaps, but I told you I was an idealist!

Often my dreams and schemes are about changing social conditions, the rights of wildlife or politics – any issue that allows me to feel part of the call for collective change. As for myself, I don't particularly want to change. Preferring to transform my friends by my presence, giving advice and showing them how to live, I am quite happy to stay the way I am.

I prefer friendship any day to 'being in love'. Love is so inconsistent, whereas friendship seems to last longer. Being in love is hard work, and demands are usually made on you right from the beginning, which is totally against my nature. So my ideal partner has to be my friend. Friends accept you the way you are and don't try to change you. There are no conditions, and trust is genuine. Human passions and emotional blackmail prevent me from feeling love in the truest sense of the word. To me, human love is about giving and accepting another human being for who they are, not making demands or expecting them to match your high expectations.

Essentially, I want to be understood and valued for

my own highly liberal, humanitarian beliefs, accepted for my strong convictions and my, albeit sometimes maverick, morality. This may not always coincide with the ethics of others, or even the country in which I live and its politics, but my own sense of right and wrong, injustice and justice is very valuable to me. If a friend or partner can understand and share all these inner values with me, then they'll be loved for life!

The element of Water

Your inner energy is intuitive and adaptable

Water in the environment

Traditionally, Water is associated with the Black Palace of the Tortoise, the north and winter.

Water is fluid and symbolic of all energy that flows and moves with instinct and with reflection. Water is either in motion or apparently still, yet the ripples on a pond or the undercurrents of a calm sea remind us that Water has no shape, instead adapting and blending around form. Water is the origin of all living things: oceans once covered the earth, and we are born in a womb filled with fluid that nourishes and protects us. Throughout ancient mythologies Water is the creative source from which all life began. It is both the life-force and the power of cosmic energy.

We are surrounded by Water in our natural environment, from the rain that falls upon our umbrellas, the great seas and the tiniest dew-ponds, to the composition of our own bodies. Without Water we would not exist. We depend upon it for life, as we do upon the air that we breathe. Water is elusive, it cannot be held, which is why it is concerned with intuition, psychic energy and the ability to see the past, present and the future as one uncaptured moment. For, like Water, we cannot hold time in our hands.

A Water's eye view

My need to communicate is probably what sets me apart from everyone else. I have to find out about everything in life, which is why I flow and adapt to each circumstance or experience that comes my way. Some people find this flexibility hard to accept, but for me, staying rigidly fixed to one opinion or way of life means you lose out on an awful lot. My problem is that I am also deeply sensitive. So sensitive to other people's moods and feelings that I think they sometimes merge with my own. This means I never know whether what I am feeling is coming from the real me! This also creates an identity problem. Finding out who I really am is one big quest in my life. I often get told I'm fickle or inconsistent, but this is only because I must continually change scenarios, plans and ideas just in case I catch up with the elusive side of me. Funny that.

Friends and family think I'm pretty elusive anyway. But I need to flow, I need to move and adapt, keeping things transient rather than immobile!

I love conversation, words and gossip. No one else can really keep up with my need for chatter, and I can irritate my friends because I never stop talking. But there's one thing I am good at – and that's listening to other people's problems. Its odd, but most of my friends come to me as a shoulder to cry on. I quite like it. It makes me feel wanted, and gives me a sense of balance. Being so neurotic about my own feelings and needs, it does me good to listen to other people's problems. I am often told that I would make a good counsellor or should look for work in the helping professions. But I can get choked with so many other people's problems that I become emotionally drained and as a result become more confused about my own needs and values. Sometimes I'm described as a bit of a psychic sponge and because I understand emotional problems all too well, I often end up carrying everyone else's grief or sorrow around for them. Then I get restless and want to escape! To the countryside or the sea, I don't mind. Both suit my gentle and intuitive nature. In such environments, I have the chance to clear my head. Although the idea of being totally alone is abhorrent to me, I get confused and anxious in towns and cities. So a quiet rural environment combined with frequent trips to the centre of town would suit me best!

My home would have to be light and filled with romantic images, books, soft lighting, candles and music.

I can be quite persuasive when I know what I want. And if this should be a romantic encounter, I can also be very seductive. Apparently changing my mind and going along with what someone else wants, I'll keep coming back to my own needs in quite an artful way. Friends have told me that I can both talk my way out of, and into, any situation! Somehow, I can always think of a way out of trouble. That's why people often ring me up for advice. I love talking on the phone, but I may be not awfully good at listening on it if I've got something of my own to worry about.

I like to be youthful and want to enjoy the romance and passion of being in love. I don't want to be tied down too soon, maybe not at all. I enjoy flirting and then finding someone else to impress with my wit and charm. This stems not so much from fickleness as a need to try as many partners as I possibly can. How else will I know when the right person comes along? Appearing passive and unfocused, I sometimes get myself into deep water. People think I'm an easy catch, because, being Water, I seem dreamy and disorganized. Then I have to use my extraordinary imagination to get myself out of tricky moments. And I usually do. It's a skill, but if you're a romantic like me, this kind of thing happens often.

Being so clever sometimes causes resentment. I don't mean to be cunning or crafty – it just seems that way because I have to defend myself from entrapment. Partners have a hard time keeping up with my quick-witted brain and highly potent imagination. But life's harsh side – all the sadness and horror in the world, and the cruelty of mankind – really disturbs my fragile feelings. So I am always looking for ways to enjoy a breath of fresh air, or to find beauty in the landscape or on the walls of an art gallery.

I'm usually very creative. It's a way of expressing my feelings, and releasing all that choked up pain and anger I often feel about the world. I'm talented at music, and usually have a good ear. Music and art must be part of my everyday life, and if I don't make use of them in my home, I may well be involved in some creative kind of work. I can write poetry and inspiring stories. If you put a canvas in front of me I may not know how to use oils, but I'll learn quicker than anyone else. Versatility is one quality I wouldn't be without. This means, of course, that it's hard for me to devote myself exclusively to one subject. I want to touch everything there is.

Painfully aware of every change in the environment, I often become paranoid and hypercritical if things don't feel comfortable. If the weather isn't right, I can whip myself into a terrible state trying to decide what to wear, and then get neurotic if I can't change when the temperature alters again. I need to adapt to the environment like a chameleon! If only I had the power to change colour and not worry about the logistics behind it every morning! I may find it difficult to commit myself to a partner or lover, but it's even harder to decide on the clothes I may be wearing in half an hour's time.

I am happiest in company. Being alone is good for me only in small doses. I am highly gregarious, which is why I often find romance waiting around every corner. It's best for me to be surrounded by people and to have an extensive network of friends, because then I don't have time to be alone. Being alone brings me nearer to the well of emotions and feelings I carry around. In a sense, I'd rather not have time to connect to my deeper

self, preferring to keep changing and reflecting whoever or whatever is out there. It's easier to ride along
with the storm than to stand against it. I'm not much of
a fighter, but I have a heart of emotional strength. You
see, being so sure that there must be more goodness
than badness out there, I tend to trust my judgement or
intuition. Usually I am right to do so, but if, on the odd
occasion, I do slip up, then I feel really hurt and suffer a
lot of pain. I hate people or things that shake my trust
and belief in universal good.

Intimate relationships can be difficult for me. As a
born-again romantic, I know what it is to fall in love. I
know how painful it is, because I've been through it
all so many times before. (I also believe in reincarna-
tion so that makes romance a million years old in my
head!) I can get addicted to falling in love, but as soon
as the initial fascination fades, I become bored and
restless or long for escape again.

People often regard me as promiscuous, and I do
enjoy many relationships, but it's only because I'm
searching for an ideal. Not many partners can really
keep up with me, as I need someone who's totally
flexible, someone who would be willing to set up camp
on a mountain one night and then spend a fortune in a
casino the next! Also I don't like heavy emotional
scenes. Intellectual and mental stimulation, wining and
dining, talk and more talk are what really turn me on.
I hate to commit myself, only because I might change
my mind and then appear inconsistent and unpredictable. I suffer from tunnel vision when it comes to
love – I just assume this is it! Forming attachments so
easily means I don't rationalize or consider the situation or the consequences carefully enough. I've been

known to fall in love with a book, a painting or a house just as easily as with a partner, which is what makes my life so risky at times. I don't always think things through and end up finding myself involved with someone or something that soon has little true meaning for me.

What I need to try to discover are my true values in life: what exactly I want from a relationship, and whether it's right for me before jumping in at the deep end! I can be as impulsive as a Fire person, but I don't have the dynamic egocentricity that enables Fire to mobilize the relationship in the right direction or to get out of it if it's not going anywhere. In reality, I find it hard to follow through my ideas when they fail to live up to their initial promise.

Friends often tell me I must be psychic, and that's fine when I'm not thinking about it. But as soon as I try to be psychic I lose touch with intuitive feelings and end up just relying on my powerful imagination, which is not the same thing. As a child I had incredible psychic power, although I wasn't really aware of what it was at the time.

As I grow older, it becomes harder to connect to that place again. Essentially, I have to feel my way through life, trust my intuition and use my incredible ability to back myself up with logic when I really find life testing me. I can be flexible and astute enough when I really allow my brain to work and don't just follow the irrationality of my unfocused mind. I'm a survivor, for all my sensitivity.

The element of Fire

Your inner energy is potent and passionate

Fire in the environment

Traditionally, Fire is associated with summer, the colour red, the Phoenix and the south.

Fire is active, dynamic energy. It is the potency of life, the very essence of beginnings and the first impulsive foot on our journey. Fire ascends and burns. It produces light and awareness. Once it was only the gods who knew the secret of Fire, but it was given to mankind and symbolizes the instigation of all that we do.

Although Fire is a stimulating element, too much of it can scorch us. Fire can produce flames that move too fast, like a forest fire that rages out of control and destroys all in its path. But Fire also warms us and melts snow and cold hearts. The summer is filled with heat and our lives are replete with passion and fantasy – the fires of human desire. Without Fire we would not have warmth in our lives and would find it difficult to survive. Fire is created from Wood: when you first rub two sticks together you realize how the spark of energy is formed. So Fire also represents that spark of inspiration, that moment of incitement, of daring, of our willingness to take a risk.

Fire is the moment within us that works without logic, without forethought. It looks only to the future, and it sees the present or the past as being of little significance. It sometimes burns others without thinking of the consequences, which is why Fire must be handled with care.

A Fire's eye view

I'm passionate about life and proud of it. There is so much to learn about in the world and a million places to go. Quite honestly, and I am exceedingly honest (sometimes against my better judgement), the bigger the adventure and the wider the horizon, the more I enjoy life. Freedom and fun are the two essential components of my way of being. I just have to get up and go if my enthusiasm suddenly lifts me off the ground. That's what it feels like anyway. I've always wanted to run before I could walk. Now I want to get straight to the heart of things and believe that my way is the right way. Friends tell me I'm self-centred and vain, but you've got to have courage and motivation in this world if you want to get anything done. So, I'm very strong about myself and I know it. I don't have much time for slobs or wimps. I need friends, family and lovers to be as optimistic and provocative about life as I am.

I get quite impatient with the mundane things in life. Cooking, cleaning, mending things or changing a punctured tyre are all liable to make me angry. I have no time for inanimate objects unless they are functional and work. If it doesn't work, chuck it out! Everything is urgent in this world, and I need to get on to the next problem rather than dwell in the past. Because I have this childlike quality, I want everything now, and get very pushy about it, I sometimes make more enemies than friends. I don't mean to be so demanding; it's just that I like to move faster than most people, and I really can't stand waiting around for anything or anyone. I've been known to stamp my feet and leave my friends behind if they can't keep up with my extraordinary energy. Activity is what I need. No sitting around in some pub all night. I want action, the great outdoors or the biggest adventure possible.

I have a great vision, though, of how things should be in life. Some people even comment about how inspirational I can be. For all my arrogance, I can generate a lot of energy in others, firing them up so they really believe they can conquer whatever goal they've set their hearts on. You see I'm a believer, an eternal optimist who knows that if you really have faith in your objectives in life you can usually achieve them.

Of course, life is not without its struggles. For all my courage, big talk and exuberance about where I'm going, I'm actually quite vulnerable inside. Because I'm so proud I try not to show it. I have to protect myself first, and others second. This sounds egotistic, but if I'm safe, then my friends and family can always rely on me. Honesty is important to me. I never twist the truth, and I always say what I feel. Bluntness can hurt, but at least I never lie. If I get things wrong, well then it's usually because I don't think long about anything, and so may make mistakes. I don't mean to be personal, but sometimes my friends think I'm too vain about my thoughts, lifestyle and ideas.

Always making up my own mind means I never

pay much attention to anyone else. This is why I sometimes find it difficult to sustain close relationships. I need someone who needs their freedom and respects mine too. No emotional leeches for me!

I know I'm exhausting to have around, but I'm also incredibly loyal. If you can't keep up with my sudden plans to hike around the Himalayas or spend a wild weekend in New York, then I won't wait for you. I have to take the plunge and go, whether you want to come or not. There's no time to analyse and dissect ideas and plans with me around. I have to be passionate about the future, because the world is a big place and I've got to see it all.

My one big problem, and I'll admit this, is that I often find out too late how rash I can be. Jumping in where others fear to tread means that I don't always consider the consequence of my actions. Well actually, never, if I'm honest. Trail-blazing and restless daring may be enviable to some, but it does lead me into difficult situations and means that I experience many disappointments as well as joys in my life.

I don't believe in competition. Now that may sound odd because I'm always out there competing; whether in sport or big business, I want to be where the action is, I want to be first. But competition for me is not about winning and losing but about getting on with the action and forging your way to the end for your own sense of achievement. Other people don't matter too much. If they get to the top first, then I might be angry, but I'll just get there by a different route. It seems to me that if you run into trouble on the way and have to fight off a few adversaries, well, all the more fun!

At work I can be exasperating, because I come up

with great ideas and expect them to happen instantly. If the plan doesn't get off the ground with the speed of Concorde then I become restless and impatient and really get on everyone's nerves. I don't understand why other people can't live at my speed. This means that I am usually the organizer or the leader in any working environment. To be part of a team would give me too many sleepless nights. I'm too impatient to hang around for bureaucratic decisions to be made, and meetings and corporate machinations make me shudder. I'd rather be out there on my own selling myself than worrying about the costings involved. If I can be in charge, I know everything will work and that taking a few risks is going to get me to the top. If I don't get instant answers or results, I'll often drop the whole scheme and think up something new. Creating a new fruit for the tree is far more exciting and challenging than waiting for old apples to ripen.

In close relationships I really want someone who's as excited about life as me, and perhaps can admire me, too. I adore passion and have an extraordinary ability to remain faithful if the right person comes along. I need my freedom, but I also need to be loved for it. If my partner can't accept my need for a fairly dramatic lifestyle, then I won't be around long. Passive, introverts aren't my type, but I sometimes find myself intrigued by them, falling madly in love and out again just as quickly!

The problem is that because quiet, dreamy types are so very different from myself I want to be near them. I'm so intrigued by such differences that I can get quite passionate about it for a while. But unfortunately it soon wears off and I have to make my escape.

This means, of course, that I get a reputation for being audacious and self-centred. But again, it's really all about pride. I have such great expectations to live up to, that I can't allow myself to fall beneath them. Warm, feeling people may open up my emotional bubble, and then my vulnerable side will be revealed for all the world to see. But worst of all as soon as I see that weak side of myself, I'll run!

I love people with a brilliant sense of humour. Laughing is as good as sex, and if you can't amuse me then I'll get bored and leave. I'm also pretty funny myself when I choose to be. If I can keep laughing, moving and enjoying life, then there's not much else I'll demand from it. Unfortunately, there aren't many people around who can relate to such an easy way of life. All I seem to do is meet complicated people dragging around their heavy emotional baggage. Relationships are crucial to my well-being. I'm not a hermit, but I'm so passionate about life that it seems crazy to be pessimistic. I like provoking others. It's fun. But the fun is about amusing myself, not about upsetting anyone.

Unfortunately, these are the sort of risks that lead me into troubled waters! All I want to do is inspire people to enjoy themselves. Why worry about yesterday when you can enjoy today and plan for tomorrow? But don't think you can fence me in. Without the wide-open spaces of experience and dramatic living, I'd be like a dampened firework about to go out. Then, I'd fizzle and go off when you least expected it. Excitement and passion are for me, whatever the cost!

The element of Earth

Your inner energy is grounded and sensual.

Earth in the environment

The traditional Feng Shui associations for Earth are the centre, late summer (the Earth season), yellow and the emperor.

The Earth is the nourisher of all things, and is concerned with our seasons, the natural rhythms of the world, the moon, the sun and the stars. Earth is also the place where we live, and from which our own inventions of time and matter and our sense of reality have been born. Earth is about the here and now, and the boundaries we create for ourselves and for others. It wants to make the abstract useful, and to manifest ideas and feelings on the material plane. Earth is associated mostly with what comes from the ground (apart from precious metal), such as stones, pebbles, rocks and crystals.

Earth is about the ability to observe the world without judgement, to watch the landscape, the changes of time and the cyclic renewal after death that transforms the seasons, our lives and the earth itself. Earth people are probably more in tune with nature than any one else, for they can listen, see, touch and feel with a sense of the ground beneath them. They are conscious spectators of the unfolding drama of life. Earth energy is ancient, but it sets out to bring the present into focus rather than dwell on the past. Because Earth is the central point from which all compass points radiate, it resonates most easily with all the other elements and their corresponding colours and seasons.

An Earth's eye view

What I enjoy most about life is the pleasure of living. Although life is not always good, if good experiences come my way I can really indulge in the moment without worrying about the future or the past. I am so sensually in tune with the world that I can just delight in touching a blade of grass, dipping my toes in the sea or feeling the trickle of water across the palm of my hand. These are idyllic experiences, but I'm also ready for the harsh side of reality. Perhaps because I am so prepared for the difficulties it means I really appreciate the people and experiences in life that give me pleasure.

Grounded as I am, I can see how others have problems coping with life, especially if they have no sense of their own value. Sometimes, when I meet friends or acquaintances who don't value their security or who live precariously, I begin to worry about my own needs. Being self-aware is an important issue for me. I am extremely aware of which friends I value and the lifestyle that makes me feel comfortable, and I want my friends, family and partners to have the same serious intentions about their quality of life, too.

Inner and outer security are crucial aspects of my life. But being so resilient means that I sometimes find it hard to adapt or change anything in my life for fear of feeling vulnerable and defenceless. Then I just become a nervous wreck rather than face the inevitability of having to change something! Many people say I'm just stubborn, that I resist change and the opinions of others because I'm weak and can't face coming out of my nice safe shell. But I enjoy my tenacity, because at least then I can observe the world from a vantage point of a reliable sanctuary, one that many might wish they had!

I can seem disturbingly cautious to those who don't know me well. But that's because I don't trust people easily, and it explains why I take a long time to make a close relationship. However, once I do, I'm committed.

I never, never chase after anyone. Whether in romance, mere acquaintance or deeper friendship, I prefer to let others come to me first. They have to be quite persuasive to get me to follow their way of thinking, as preservation and survival of self are my immediate concerns. This feels like a kind of instinctive energy at work in me, and explains why I can seem so indulgent and incredibly possessive about my home, my family and my partner. I'll hang on desperately to what I value, because if something is worthy of my investment, then it deserves to be nurtured and cared for. I like to surround myself with many possessions, and I'm quite acquisitive when I discover objects or beautiful things in life that touch my soul. Art and music are extremely important to me, and I like to live somewhere that is aesthetically pleasing, preferably filled with wonderful antiques or at least with rich colours and exotic fabrics.

I'm not really afraid of anything. I don't worry about the future, because I love living in the here and now. Yes, I may seem pragmatic and irritatingly capable, but as long as I trust my instincts you'll always have a loyal friend or partner. The friends who accept me for who I am know that my solidity is as valuable as gold.

At work my colleagues know I'm an excellent administrator, who works well behind the scenes. What they don't know is how jealous I can become if others reach their goals before me. This is not because I want what they have – I'm materialistic only because I like to be comfortable. Things have to feel right, otherwise I'm a total mass of insecurities! I am quite intuitive about people, and often find friends drawn to me because they feel safe, or they know I can make them feel good about themselves. It's not that I inspire them with great ideals; rather I provide a sense of solidity, grounding their dreams, and providing them with the security that allows them to trust me with their secrets.

I feel very deeply. My emotions are strong and sometimes lead me into terrible scenes with others. Yes, my stubbornness is my best and worst friend. It's useful when work needs to be finished, or I must find the determination to succeed at something others would give up on. But when I'm feeling really pigheaded, I won't give up on anything, especially if the alternative means admitting I could possibly be wrong! The problem is that because I want to be right,

I usually assume I am, then dig myself into a pit and refuse to budge.

Family and friends, lovers and partners are all invaluable to me, but I am also very self-reliant. The bare necessities of life are all I need. Food, sex, good company, nature, birds singing, music playing – simple and wholesome things. I have the reputation for being rather self-indulgent and hedonistic at times. But you have to enjoy the moment and the pleasures of life, and these won't come to you of their own accord: you have to go out and get them.

I'm often told that I have a good speaking and singing voice, and that I'm also quite artistic because I can relate to natural beauty and the sensuality of creativity. I need loads of affection. Hugging and kissing, touching and being tickled. It's not necessarily sexual, so much as sensual.

I find it difficult to accept sudden changes, because anything that can turn around so fast seems unworthy of deeper attention. I need to make absolutely sure that things will work out for the best. Slow change is OK, but impulsive actions just don't fit my tortoise shell.

Acutely sensitive to pretentiousness and arrogance, I won't waste time getting to know someone or cultivating a new circle of friends if it doesn't feel right to me. I trust my senses, after all. This is the primitive and instinctual side of my nature and goes some way to explaining why the human race has survived so long. Some people think primitive means stupid, but it can also mean first, the first to really know the truth about being!

If you're in trouble I'll be the first to calm you

down, offer advice and give you a sense of reality. I'm receptive and nurturing, and genuinely enjoy caretaking. I am often described as serene, a sort of calm water for other people's breakers. Yet being so patient and tolerant can also make me frightened that I'll be alone one day. I often get left or abandoned once I've sorted out everyone else's problems. The future is not something I really think about, which explains why I'm not very good at accepting that people and events must move on.

At work I'm not considered particularly ambitious, but if I fix on an opening or a job that would improve my status and material comforts, I'll be determined to succeed. The hard part is losing. So often I wait until the very last minute to put my self forward or to offer my services, and then its usually too late because some smarter, quicker, more spontaneous genius has already taken the opportunity. My caution can be my downfall.

Relationships are quite difficult for me. I need a partner who's mysterious, someone quiet rather than extrovert, although I often fall for dramatic, fiery types, just because they are so exciting. But essentially I need someone who can share my love of nature and the good things of life. They must accept my introspective side, when I need to walk across the hills or along the seashore in moments of solitary attunement with nature. After such a commune with Mother Earth, I'm ready to return to close companionship. Relationships are important to me, because I've got so much affection and love to offer. Love means sharing everything! Some people say I'm undoubtedly the most sensual and sexual of all the elements, but I haven't really noticed. I do love baths, massages and bodies though!

Partners may find me a bit selfish, but I am never disloyal or unpredictable in return. Rather, I'm what you'd call a safe bet when it comes to long-term relationships. Once I've made up my mind, then that's it. But I can be unbearably pragmatic and often jealous, so anyone who can't live with this rather clingy side of me, won't be around for long. I don't mean to be jealous, but sometimes a terrible fear of rejection overwhelms me – the source of my real insecurity. Being loved and liked is just as important for me as loving others. If anyone criticizes me, I'm sure to take it the wrong way. I'm so reactive that at times I sit for hours wondering why I've hurt someone, or what I've done to upset them! By the time I've worked out what to say, it's usually too late to make amends. Patience is a virtue they say, but for me patience also means tolerance. I am incredibly tolerant of what feeds me, and intolerant of what does not. And I always know which is which! At least I'm not fickle or indecisive. I know what I want, and I know even if it takes for ever to get it, I'm about the only kind of person around with the credibility and determination to do it!

The element of Metal

Your inner energy is ambitious and single-minded

Metal in the environment

The traditional associations for Metal are the tiger, the west, silver, white and the autumn.

Metal is forged from the earth's surface, the result both of the gradual solidification of the Earth over time (producing the metals we know in the natural world, such as gold, iron, zinc, platinum and tin) and man-made effort. This is why Metal represents the power of knowledge and the transmission of information. Metal puts abstract concepts into reality. For the Chinese, Metal was primarily symbolic of gold and thus represented wealth and power. Highly auspicious as gold and silver are, they are rarely found in our environment and must be handled with care.

A Metal's eye view

They say I'm the most extreme of all the elements and that's probably true. I find myself lurching from self-pity and melancholy to extraordinary arrogance and optimism! This reflects my ability to regenerate when I'm feeling at my lowest. I can plunge into the depths of despair over the most ridiculous slight, but then once

I've re-dedicated myself to the purpose behind my feelings, I can quite quickly bounce back to my more exciting self. Some people say I'm charismatic and enjoy my company; others really hate me – the way I seem so in control of myself. That's only because I really fear anyone getting close enough to see my vulnerable side. There's a kind of icy exterior to everything I do, but inside I suffer an awful lot from a sense of isolation.

To make up for this, I organize everyone. I'm good at that. I like to feel that I'm the one who can sort out any crisis with my ingenuity and incredible sense of responsibility. Being so serious about life takes its toll on me, though, and I often need to take a break from the strong demands I place on myself. To be able to function efficiently in work and in my relationships is the most positive boost to my well-being, but if my friends or colleagues are faint-hearted, they'll never be able to keep up with me!

I can usually tell whether or not a new idea at work will succeed – an ability that reflects my shrewd and astute nature. Equally, I'm determined to succeed where my future is at stake. Yes, I do admit to being ambitious, and I'm not scared of hard work. But I can be a loner and choose to go my own way rather than following the herd or the team. I'm probably better at lone sports, like mountaineering or yachting, or battling with my own ego and beating my own times rather than competing with others. I don't really enjoy sharing responsibility with others, either. The trouble is I'm so sure that my way is the only one, and the best, that if anyone else does it differently I can be totally inflexible and vindictive.

I can always see what's going on in other people's

hearts and minds. It's not intuition – it's more like having X-ray vision – and even my best friends think I'm creepy sometimes when I have instant awareness of what's going on.

But I do feel isolated inside. Sometimes this lonely part of me wants to reach out and grab someone, but I'm so secretive and single-minded that I'd rather retreat into a book or hide in the shadows than make a fool of myself. I know what I want, and I can be incredibly compulsive about my desires. Not just sexual ones, either! Getting to the top in any profession or career is perhaps what suits me best. This goes for relationships, too – I like to be the instigator. Once I am involved with someone though, I'm probably the most loyal of any of the elements. My integrity is unique and there are few who can criticize it.

When I put my intuition to work and take a risk that others wouldn't dare to, I'm usually proved right. But this can get me into trouble with my friends and family. They don't realize that my dedication is infallible and that my decisions are based on an appreciation of the consequences of any action, not just on possibilities. Gut reactions speak to me, yes, but logical reasoning has to be part of the process of making plans as well.

My friends can usually rely on me for advice, and as I'm not fickle nor the least bit interested in gossip, I can keep the biggest secrets in the world. My own values are based on integrity and my continued success. If I cannot be relied on to be someone's confidant, then I would have to reconsider my own standing. Sometimes this makes me seem arrogant, interested only in my own autonomy. But I do desperately want to share my life with an equal partner.

In relationships I like to be in charge, or at least feel that both of us have a separate identity. That means we have our own careers, and socialize with our own groups of friends as well as with each other's. I can be quite ruthless about my partners. If for any reason they undermine my power, I am quite likely to dump them. Once a relationship has ended, for whatever reason and even if it's my own fault, there's usually no going back. Whether I've made a mistake or been slighted makes no difference. I cut myself off completely from the past, because survival is based on starting afresh.

Some people never get to understand me, nor will they ever get close enough. I suppose the darker side of life is something I find fascinating, and I can guide anyone into these shadowy lands, because I know them so well myself. For me, a crisis is always a turning point, a chance for regeneration and a new phase in my life. I seem to have experienced so many moments of loss in my life that I'm used to it. Maybe that's why I seem so cool and insensitive. But I've learned the hard way, and I know how easy it is to abuse power, particularly my own.

It's not that I haven't got a sense of humour, but I tend to find life a serious business. When I was a child I don't think anyone paid much attention to me, because I was a bit of a loner, quiet and fairly shy. Now I'm grown up, I feel mature and worldly wise, and I need friends and relationships that sparkle and lighten my sense of responsibility and duty. I'm not without feelings though. You know, when I'm hurt, I really hurt. But this doesn't mean that I have to show it! What I usually do when I feel wounded is either to retaliate so fast that the other person doesn't even have time to think, or totally let go. Sometimes I will just disappear out of people's lives for ever. I need to do it, to allow my feelings to be felt and acknowledged.

What I love about life is climbing to the top of a mountain. It's the thrill of knowing that my single-mindedness will pay off in the end. To be so determined can put people's backs up, but I keep going, indomitable, until I get there.

In close relationships sex is very important to me. I am highly sexed, and can be quite demanding. The problem is that I'm unwilling to give up my independence and my solitude too easily. A permanent one-to-one relationship could work, but I'd have to be absolutely certain that I could maintain my own lifestyle. This might well conflict with a partner's needs, who may find me too self-centred, when actually I just want to get on with living my life to the full. No apron strings, no sad chords, no heartaches. It's too painful.

Mind you, I have my moments of sheer self-indulgent melancholy. Life can't always be filled with achievement, and there are times when I turn into a depressed and victimized weakling. However, this can be quite healthy for me, because I usually regenerate and pull myself together, even stronger for the experience. Friends find it impossible to handle me when I'm like this, and perhaps I'm best left alone. In fact, periods of loneliness can be creative for me. Often my best schemes for the future are born in my darkest moments of self-pity! Still, I want to be loved just like any other person, and as long as I'm respected for my integrity, for my personal space and my freedom, then I can be the most loyal magnetic and dedicated of partners.

Chapter Two

The Elemental Phases

Now you know the essence of your birth element energy, you may find that it does not seem relevant to your current lifestyle, relationships, work or personality. This is because we all go through cycles of change in our outer world. Our perception changes, as does our environment. So although you may be a Fire element by birth, you may find you are currently feeling like a Water person, or even expressing Metal energy! To find out which is your current dominant or key element, use the elemental statements below to determine which phase you are currently going through.

Identifying with one element will help you to focus on the major influences and energies you are currently experiencing in your life, and what you can do to enjoy complete inner and outer harmony in this phase. Once you have established which element is the most influential *now*, read the suggestions under that section that appear later in this chapter. Consider the statements as honestly as you can. The questionnaire can be accurate only if you honour your feelings and listen to your heart.

How to discover your key element

In each of the sections on the following pages there are ten statements for you to consider. Read each one carefully and decide which ones resonate with your current lifestyle and which ones don't. Give each statement a score on the following scale of -1 to 3:

-1   No – unimaginable ever!

 0   No – I can't relate to this at the present time

 1   This is only occasionally true

 2   This is often true

 3   Yes – I have a very strong resonance to this now

Once you have worked your way through all the statements, add up your scores using the Scoring chart (page 61) to see which is your dominant, or key, element.

Intimate relationships

a   I prefer a partner who totally respects my independence.

b   My kind of lover must be as passionate about life as me!

c   I need someone who is affectionate, capable and nurturing.

d   I like partners who are humanitarian and socially adept.

e   I prefer my partner to be unpredictable and witty.

f   Sexually, I prefer to be in control.

g   I can be quite experimental, but sex has to be sophisticated.

h   I am extremely sensual and don't like to be rushed!

i   Sexually, I am daring and often impulsive.

j   I can be shy about my body and find it difficult to really let go.

Body/diet/fitness

a   I always make sure I eat a balanced diet.

b   I think I'm healthy, so I don't worry about what I eat.

c   Most meals are haphazard – just when I feel like it.

d   I usually follow a strict regime – my body is special.

e   I love indulging myself in all the things I'm not supposed to eat!

f   Exercise means I can keep healthy and channel my nervous energy.

g   I don't have time for fitness classes; I prefer working.

h   If I want to keep fit, I'll do it with panache, jog everywhere, join every class, read every diet book.

i   Fresh air and the countryside are all I need to feel fit.

j   I usually opt for walking or cycling everywhere to be environmentally friendly.

Career/vocation

a   I am ambitious, and certain I shall succeed in my career.

b   I never know what I want to do – there's so much choice!

c   As long as I can be involved in social or humanitarian work I'll be happy.

d   I need to do something creative, even if I don't make any money.

e   I get enthusiastic about new ventures and prefer to work as an instigator, rather than as part of a team.

f   Work colleagues say I'm pushy, but I'm quick to see an opening.

g   Challenges are what motivate me, as long as
     they keep me inspired.

h   Although I'd rather work for a cause, I can find
     one in any workplace.

i   I'd like to have a career that involves beautiful
     things, like paintings, interiors or music.

j   I want to experience all sorts of things in life,
     so it's really difficult to make up my mind.

Environment/holidays

a   I feel happiest with a book and my own
     company.

b   I need to be outside in the wide open spaces:
     plenty of fresh air, mountains and the sea.

c   I love crowded restaurants brimming with
     chatting and laughing faces, where there is an
     abundance of wine and food.

d   Travelling, driving from one place to another,
     flying from city to city and being on the move
     are essential to me.

e   I'd prefer to indulge in a luxurious bath, be
     massaged and have stimulating dinner parties.

f   All I need is a beach, the sun and wonderful
     wine.

g   I'd join a course about astrology, acupressure
     or aromatherapy – anything that stimulates my
     mind with like-minded people.

h   Far from the madding crowd for me – on the highest mountain or the loneliest island, away from everyone.

i   A Caribbean island with endless water sports, an exciting night life and lots of fun.

j   A trip up the Amazon, a safari in Africa or a hike round the Himalayas would suit me.

Family/home

a   I would rather have a partner or share a flat. I hate being alone.

b   I prefer to live alone, or at least have a partner who allows me lots of space and a room to myself!

c   My home must be beautiful, and everything in it would be carefully chosen.

d   My home would be minimalist. I can't stand clutter, and wouldn't spend much time there anyway.

e   If I couldn't live in a gypsy caravan, then it would have to be somewhere dramatic or outrageous!

f   I don't particularly want children around; my career is more important.

g   My children would be the most special creation of my life; I'd like to think of them as my friends.

h   I don't think about having children yet; there's too much fun to have in life first.

i   The world is my home, and if I had kids they would have to share my view that the world is my family too.

j   I would pamper my children, and ensure they felt safe, secure and loved.

How to work out your elemental energy

1   Use the scoring chart (table 2) on the opposite page.

2   Work through the questions again, inserting the score you have given each statement in the element columns. You'll find the statements for each section arranged under the elements. Just enter your score in each element column.

For example:
If you gave no points for statement 'a' in the Relationship section, then insert zero next to 'a' and so on, as below:

	Fire	Earth	Metal	Water	Wood
Relationships	b = 0	c = 3	a = 0	e = 2	d = -1

Table 2: Scoring chart

	Fire	Earth	Metal	Water	Wood
Relationships	b =	c =	a =	e =	d =
	i =	h =	f =	j =	g =
Body/fitness	b =	e =	d =	c =	a =
	h =	i =	g =	f =	j =
Career	e =	d =	a =	b =	c =
	g =	i =	f =	j =	h =
Environment	d =	e =	b =	c =	a =
	i =	f =	h =	g =	j =
Family/home	e =	c =	d =	a =	b =
	h =	j =	f =	g =	i =

TOTAL

Now add up your scores for each element column. Whichever element score comes out highest is your dominant or key element right now. However, if two elements have the same top score, then read both elemental phase sections and decide which you feel most affinity with.

If you have a good balance of elements, then just use your Birth element as your key. If, however, you have an extremely undeveloped element, i.e. one with a very low score, then it can be helpful to read about its characteristics to establish what benefits of this energy might be missing in your life.

Remember, each elemental phase has been divided into a Light phase and a Dark phase. There are times when we are caught up in the positive qualities of the elemental energy and life seems full of joy; at other times we are forced to deal with the more negative modes of expression, when our lives are going through crises, pain or conflict.

It is helpful to read the characteristics of both the Light and Dark Phases and decide which of these applies most to you.

Once you have read your relevant section, go straight to the corresponding elemental palace chapter to find ways to improve and bring harmony to all aspects of your life.

If you are going through a Wood element phase

Light

You may find yourself drawn to unconventional people, that you become more rebellious than usual or want to make expansive changes that will affect everyone around you. Bizarre events might occur and you may find yourself involved in social or political issues which normally don't appeal to you. The big questions about what life is all about and what is happening to the world may become more challenging and important to you than individual issues. Close, personal friendships begin to seem unnecessary, and you may prefer the company of many rather than the intimacy of a few.

You may become highly sociable, go to more parties, take up country pursuits or join humanitarian groups. You may feel detached from your feelings, preferring to rationalize objectives rather than taking notice of gut reactions or intuition. You may want to perfect your environment, be drawn to colours and styles of clothes that normally you might find outrageous and eccentric. This is a time of vision and practicality, a time when belonging to the collective is more satisfying and rewarding than self-aggrandizement; but it is also a time when you must retain your independence and ideals at all costs.

Dark

Relationships may prove difficult. Your partner may seem possessive or over-demanding. You may need more freedom, and get the urge to travel, to discover new experiences and places alone. Others may eye you with suspicion, especially as you perhaps seem more opinionated and awkward than usual. They may accuse you of becoming arrogant about your altruism, but, inspired by your own ideals and visions, you won't really have time to listen to them. Although by spreading yourself thinly, you might make many acquaintances, you then expect to change their whole outlook on life with your own ideas. There will be moments when you seem able to translate every abstract concept into reality, and the future seems filled with endless possibilities both for yourself and the world.

This is a time when your freedom is paramount and you are not prepared to take responsibility for other people's feelings. The bigger issues suddenly assume huge importance, while the role of individuals deserves little of your attention. Others perhaps find your liberal views irritating, and you may involve yourself in confrontations where your demand is for liberty over compromise.

If you are going through a Metal phase

Light

You may have an overwhelming sense of achievement in anything you are about to embark upon, as if almost any impossible mission will have a successful and lucrative outcome. It is your vehement belief that only you can scale that particular mountain peak. Inspired by a profound sense of integrity, you begin to feel that you truly know yourself and understand your motives and objectives in life. You may put yourself in a position of power, where you can ensure that others will benefit as well as yourself. Instigating new ideas at work, or among the family, could provide a sense of new-found autonomy. Indeed, you may appear to others more determined than ever, setting new goals for yourself that can only improve your financial and emotional well-being.

Partners may find you exciting and magnetic. Luring and attracting without knowing why, you nevertheless maintain a sense of secrecy and detachment, feeling comfortable in your aloneness. You may be more sexually demanding, but you won't assume others to be less worthy than yourself, and you will uphold your own sense of purpose in line with others' needs. Every flower will smell sweeter than before, food may intoxicate your senses, as will fine wines and other luxuries, as you discover an urge for the very best in life. You may find that, for once, money doesn't slip between your fingers, and your clothes and appearance take on a refined and elegant grace. You may find you seek great transformation.

Dark

You may feel acutely extreme in everything you do, you may find yourself drawn into emotional scenes with partners just to prove you are right. You may feel compelled to make a sweeping change in your life, one that could cost you a partner or a lifestyle that has meant a lot to you.

Others may find you secretive and suspect you are hiding something, when in fact you just can't find the words to express yourself. Family and friends may insist you've become melancholic, and you may feel depressed and dejected about life and your career or profession. There will be moments when you are unable to tolerate others and be unbending in your decisions or convictions. Wine will smell unusually pungent, and your food and your local stores may not be able to supply the quality of goods you demand.

Even the company of best friends may fail to live up to your high expectations and ideals. You may feel uncomfortable in the countryside and seek only to be alone with your thoughts, or engage in a fast-paced lifestyle that gives you no time to reflect on your feelings or fears.

If you are going through an Earth element phase

Light

You may feel more centred than usual, finding a genuine need for peace and a serene lifestyle more attractive than a diversity of interests. Others may regard you as affectionate, nurturing and supportive in a calm and down-to-earth way. You may take more interest in nature and the environment, or find you can simply enjoy life by letting yourself flow with the tide. The troubles of the past and the fears for the future may disappear, as you slip into bed each night with a sense of warmth for your partner (if you have one), for yourself and your family and friends, or even for those who normally disturb your sense of balance.

You may enjoy the pleasures of life with a new perspective. Sensuality becomes a key word, whereby everything must be touched and smelt as if for the first time, listened to with new ears. You can sense the beauty in everything, and also appreciate the uglier side that life brings with it. You may be drawn to artistic pursuits, feeling the need to create music, sing songs, go on nature trails, ramble across the mountains or witness wild sunsets in obscure countries to get as close to nature as you can. Others may find that your words convey great depth, that you appear poised and consistent in your views, unhampered by insecurity. You may seek out books and gardens rather than parties and pubs, and be more likely to take some time to indulge and pamper yourself.

Dark

You may suddenly feel that life is static, that you are neither moving forward nor enjoying the present. Overwhelmed by a sense of inertia, you may not feel like going to parties, visiting those relatives or even meeting your new friend or lover off the train. People around you may think you have become materialistic and stuck in your ways. You may experience moods of profound self-reflection and moments of unfounded jealousy and deep insecurity. You may be unnecessarily stubborn in your views and convictions and become more possessive and over-protective of your partners, family or friends, who in turn see you as emotional and indulgent. In moments of conflict and resistance, when normally you could turn away without feeling you had lost a battle, you may refuse to abdicate from your position.

You may demand more from your partner and generally feel that everyone else is dumping their problems on you, when you haven't the strength to cope with yourself, let alone sort out and placate your family quarrels. You may turn to addictive behaviour. Chocolates, alcohol and falling in love all become more attractive when you're going through a Dark Earth phase.

If you are going through a Fire elemental phase

Light

An optimistic sense of well-being may fill your days with anticipation and the belief that you can do anything. You may be able to share this vision and inspire others, so that they too become vitalized and energized by your mere presence. The world will seem full of opportunity, and there may be many times when you need to venture out on to the open road in search of your vision.

Whether you pick up a backpack and walk across your chosen landscape, or travel to some wild, passionate and remote place, challenge will be your watchword, and anyone who can't live up to your impossible expectations may find you burn through their lives like a forest fire. You may singe others with your audacity, and then simply reject them for their caution or pragmatism.

You'll light everyone's life with inspiration and enthusiasm, bouncing between feelings of wild abandon and the urge to start on a new venture, and really involving yourself in some great scheme. You become attracted to taking risks, but whatever impulse leads you on, you may find it was all worthwhile. Others may comment on how daring you have become, or how they admire your sudden need for independence and freedom.

You may experience great dreams or fantasies that are dramatic, enticing and spiritually uplifting. You want to live life to the full, and enjoy your dynamic and stylish motivation.

Dark

You may be feeling extremely impatient, irritated by how slowly things are progressing and believe that you have to do something impulsive to achieve results. Your normal ability to be logical or to sense the right moment and timing of a project is suddenly blown to pieces by an irrational and sudden desire to take a risk and leap in at the deep end.

You may need to make a dramatic change in your life, a sudden parting of the ways which you would normally never contemplate. Perhaps you are convinced that any decision you make will be the right one and fail to consider the consequences of your actions.

You may be overtly provocative, take risks in love or finance, and generally appear headstrong and extremely pushy.

You could be involved in a passionate love affair, one that you believed would never be possible. But at the same time you may not have thought about how serious and dangerous the relationship could be to your future. In work you might become suddenly ambitious for more than your usual amount of success. Manipulating and undermining to achieve your goals, you may make tactless remarks and be accused of bluntness, or of going too far. With a mind too full of fantasies about love, your career and the future, you may pay little attention to the present.

If you are going through a
Water element phase

Light

You may feel more intuitive than usual, especially about the right moment to take action or make a choice. You may excel at listening to other people's problems and take time out from your own. Everyone you meet seems to be surrounded by an aura, and you are drawn mysteriously to types of friends, lovers and work colleagues you would never have dreamed of sharing time with in the past.

The whole concept of time may seem to have changed. One minute you feel that you must commit yourself to making a change or decision about your circumstances, and the next you simply adapt. Others may call you dreamy, or airy. You might lead a highly gregarious lifestyle while going through this phase, out every night, wining and dining, falling in love with every possible lover you meet. Romance will be at a peak. You may attach yourself to someone, then next moment drop them as soon as they fail to live up to your expectations. You may find you can communicate with anyone.

Strangers, family and friends may all benefit from your insight. Some will be amazed at your ability to entertain and persuade in such a charming manner. You will find yourself in demand at parties and social events, and your self-esteem will be at a high. You'll be gregarious and beguiling, and even your eyes may take on a watery, seductive quality. This is a time when you can enchant and magically revitalize both yourself and those close to you.

Dark

Friends may say you are fickle and ambivalent, although they often find themselves telling you their deepest secrets and greatest fears. You may be emotionally stifled by everyone else's psychic energy, you may carry it around with you until you feel the need to be creative or do something wildly different just to rid yourself of its pervasive influence. You want to communicate with anyone you meet, trusting strangers and the world to see things right in the end. You may feel deeply wounded if someone cuts you down, when normally it wouldn't have meant anything to you. You may feel both impressionable and self-sacrificing. You may be drawn to conflicting opinions, saying one thing and believing another, doing one thing and thinking something else.

This dichotomy won't alarm you; strangely, it may seem comforting and easy to be unattached to one idea, person or belief. People at work may shudder at first, because you are so inconsistent and more liable to do something unpredictable than ever before. You may also be more gullible and believe everything you hear. This is a time when your instincts are sharpened, but your logical mind becomes unfocused and scattered by too many thoughts, too many choices.

At home you may become disorganized, neurotic with your possessions. You might change your clothes frequently, move the furniture and even sell it. Money may slip through your fingers too quickly, and you'll begin to feel guilty for every thing imaginable that's wrong in your work and home life.

Now you know which element is either currently influencing you or represents your dominant or key element, turn to the appropriate chapter and follow the pathway through the palace to discover how to balance and bring harmony to your life. If you are currently resonating to your own birth element, similarly turn to the corresponding palace.

Chapter Three

The Palace of Fire

Crystal: cornelian or bloodstone
Natural talisman: pine cone

First make sure you have tested whether this is currently your dominant or key element. If it is not your natural birth element, you may find that your energy changes throughout the year. If so, just move into the corresponding element palace.

The Kitchen Garden is for outer and inner beauty, your body, fitness, environment and empowerment for success and self-worth. It contains Feng Shui ways to enhance your home, including rituals, moon and chakra cycles, symbols and magical affirmations and empowerments, together with auspicious times of the year for making decisions and planning.

The Secret Chamber is the place where you can

discover what you have to offer others, and what you need to learn and develop as you go through this phase.

When you walk through the doorway into the Palace of Fire you are beginning a journey where sunlight, summer plants, seasonal fragrances and crystals can nourish your body, mind and spirit. If you are in a Fire elemental phase, you need to find out how to create and maintain harmony in your life, whether you are in a Dark Fire phase or a Light Fire phase.

The Kitchen Garden

Your physical appearance and well-being are simply outer manifestations of how you feel inside, emotionally, mentally and spiritually. Working with all three at once is not easy and you may find that it is best to concentrate on one type of energy at a time. When Fire is your dominant element at birth, you need to look at what it symbolizes and represents in your life, complementing and balancing this with the other elements. Fire can benefit from incorporating all the other four elements into the environment, but especially Wood and Earth.

Fitness

Fire, by its very nature, demands action and dynamic expression. Whether you feel you are in a Light or Dark Fire phase, it is important to allow your body to express this potent energy.

Fire people thrive on physical activity, whether rock-climbing or fast and furious sprinting down the road. In traditional Chinese astrology Fire is connected to the planet Mars. Mars is hot and assertive. By expressing your physical needs and channelling this force in a positive way you can release tensions and increase your capacity for harmony, mentally and emotionally as well as physically. Motor-racing, competitive horse-riding and athletics are suitable for expressing excessive Fire energy.

Water is the least compatible of the elements for Fire, although it may be introduced carefully. In small doses, swimming can be beneficial, but only if you are sure you can keep to swimming pools and safe places. However, don't be tempted to indulge in water sports, for Water is liable to drain you of your natural exuberance and spirit. Deep-sea diving or canoeing down the rapids are also definitely not to be recommended if you are feeling a strong connection to Fire.

Team games may give you the physical exercise you need, but you might struggle with sharing the responsibility, unless you can be the team leader or captain. Any rugged, rough and highly dynamic exercise will do just as well, and you may find you have bursts of energy at moments when others would be rather sleeping or taking a quiet stroll in the countryside. Fire people need to keep on the move, and they also like to take risks or experience dangerous situations. If there is a challenge involved, any sport or activity that tests the self will be beneficial as long as it means plenty of action.

Vitalizing the inner you during the Fivefold Year

To complement and balance high Fire energy levels, Earth and Wood remedies can be incorporated to beautify and strengthen your inner and outer body.

The Chinese have five seasons of the year, unlike our four. These are spring, summer, the Earth season, autumn and winter. Diagram 5 shows you how this relates to the five elements and to Fire in particular.

As you can see, summer is the most auspicious season of the year for Fire. This is time when you feel alive and the sun is energizing you. Symbolically the moon is high in the sky and almost full, but it is still growing, still learning and disseminating. In the Chinese Fivefold Year the summer is divided into summer and the Earth season, and it crosses over into our spring and autumn. However, the summer solstice, a few days before our 'longest day', occurs right in the middle of the summer season, and if you are aware of the rhythms and cycles of nature you will notice a subtle but profound difference at this time of year. As the change from one season to another varies from year to year, use the dates on the diagram only as rough guides. For example, if you don't feel that spring has truly arrived on 5 March, don't suddenly start doing spring work until you 'feel' the time is right. It may vary by another few days, or even a week on either side of these dates.

Each season marks a specific time for attending to your body, your environment or your inner well-being. Use the following calendar to help you. By incorporating most specifically Wood and Earth Feng

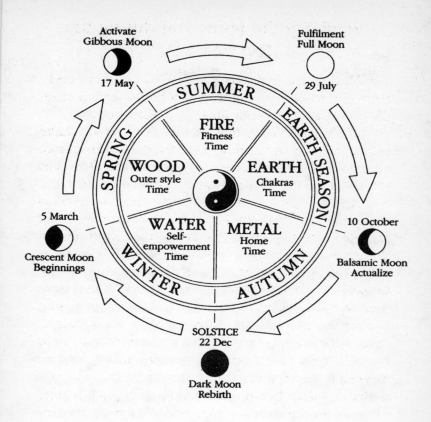

Diagram 5
The Fivefold Year for Fire

Shui enhancements and employing a more cautious use of Metal and Water aspects, you can balance your Fire element for each auspicious season.

Summer   Work with outer beauty, body, fitness and food

Earth season	Time to work with chakras for inner harmony
Autumn	Concentrate on your environment at home
Winter	Best time for working on self-empowerment
Spring	Work on outer style and inner feasts

Summer

This is a time when you can work on yourself outside, either in the sunshine or the shade. To ensure your outer beauty is in harmony with the summer, pick rosemary, mint and thyme. Use these herbs in your cooking, as they are associated with the element Wood and are good Feng Shui cures for balancing and protecting your system from the red-hot energy of Fire's often over-exuberant lifestyle. Incorporating Wood element herbs into your summer meals adds tolerance, acceptance of others and a more relaxed and altruistic attitude to the characteristic passionate self-interest of Fire.

Rosemary gives protection and nurtures, something Fire is not awfully good at providing for others. Hang a garland over your kitchen doorway to fill you with positive memories, for Fire is usually thinking about the future and refusing to reflect on the past! Don't overdo the rosemary, though, for it is quite potent.

Thyme is essential to maintain Fire's youth and childlike charm. Crush the dried herb up into tiny handfuls, fill a special terracotta pot and leave it beside your bath for added charisma if you're going out for the evening. You can cast spells with thyme: throw some across your bath-water and before you relax in the tub, remind yourself that Fire needs Wood to burn brightest and best. Your outer beauty will be greatly enhanced by an inner sense of well-being and tranquillity, no matter how fiery you intend to look when you're ready to go out!

Make herbal oils by steeping thyme or rosemary in olive oil for a few days. Use these in your cooking pot for a Wood enhancement that will balance and energize your digestive system and metabolism. A refreshing mint tea will clarify your mind.

Midsummer ritual

On Midsummer's Day, or the summer solstice, conduct a ritual with plants or herbs to bring you success and enjoyment for the coming year. Fire needs Earth to keep it stoked, so that the ashes transform, the embers glow and radiate heat. Similarly, when you are in a Fire element phase, you need to be warmed and heartened internally to ensure it is not only your outer appearance that is alive and dynamic. Fire people often burn themselves out too quickly, and this Earth ritual can generally 'slow' down Fire's excessive impulses to more acceptable levels.

Carry out the following Earth ritual either on the actual summer solstice, sunrise or sunset, or during the evenings *before* Midsummer's Day. If you are unsure of the date of the summer solstice, remember that it is also known as the 'longest day' and usually falls on 21 or 22 June – check your newspaper to make sure.

In the garden, or wherever you can be outside

under the summer sky, place two red candles (these are your Fire totems). Between them place your Earth magic: this can consist of unpolished pebbles, stones or rock crystals placed in a small terracotta or china bowl. (You must have chosen these yourself, whether from a beach, the countryside or from a selection in a shop.)

Next, gather the leaves or petals of the following plants: geranium, honeysuckle, rosemary, marigold, pinks and oak. Don't worry if you can't get hold of them all; just collect what you can. These then need to be dried. The quickest way is to spread them on a baking tray and put them in the oven for a few minutes. But if you have time, hang them in a sunny window for a few days, or place them carefully in the airing cupboard.

After they have been dried, crush them to a fine powder with a pestle and mortar, or use the back of a wooden spoon on a wooden chopping board. Don't use metal utensils for this. Metal is not a good 'blender' for your Fire ritual.

Now, sprinkle some of the powder over the stones. This melange of leaves or petals represents Fire energy. By sprinkling a few pinches on to your Earth magic, you are offering up your own energy to Earth's natural balancer.

As the sun rises or sets, use some of your Fire energy powder and sprinkle it on to the lighted flames of the candles. If you do it carefully they shouldn't be extinguished and an exquisite aroma will envelop you. As you do so, affirm to yourself: 'I am of Fire and of Fire will I burn brightly. With passion, vision, intuitive wisdom and optimism. May this clarity flow into others' hearts as well as my own, cleansing and vitalizing my body and outer beauty.'

Earth season

For Fire, this is the time of year to focus on your chakra energy. Chakra is the Sanskrit word for 'wheel'. These wheels are energy centres located at seven points that extend from the base of your spine to the top of your head. These spirals of invisible energy vibrate and reson-ate to many other energies, corresponding and relating to all aspects of our lives. By working with each chakra in turn, you can awaken yourself to more positive energy. For beauty and harmony, you need to work on sensuality and charisma. When you are in a Fire phase, or you feel a deep connection to Fire or it is your birth element, you need to work especially with the chakras that correspond to Earth and Wood (see Diagram 6).

Here is a description of the chakra energy associations at their most simplified level:

Element Earth   (Root chakra) – grounded, centred, waiting, acceptance

Element Water   (Sacral chakra) – receptive, creative, sensitive, sexual

Element Fire   (Solar Plexus chakra) – vitality, vision, enthusiasm, optimism

Element Wood   (Heart chakra) – detached love, compassion, ideals, altruism

Element Metal   (Throat chakra) – power, truth, trust, responsibility

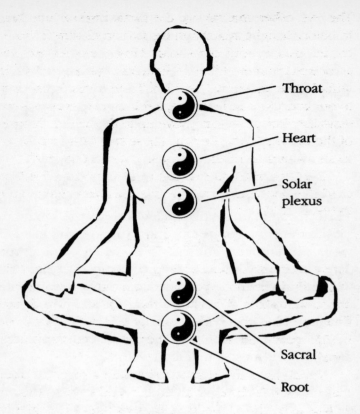

Diagram 6
The five chakras

Five other chakras have been 'discovered' more recently, but for the purposes of our elemental journey we do not need to delve further into this highly regarded system of self-understanding, growth and healing.

The two other chakras are the Brow chakra (psychic, intuition, insight, spirit) and the Crown chakra (cosmic consciousness, soul, threshold). However, they are not associated with the Chinese elements. We have to work with the five elemental chakras. These five correspond to our conscious knowledge, a self-awareness we must assimilate before we can move up to the higher chakras of the Brow and the Crown. These two bring us closer to an awareness of the unconscious, and beyond.

The two chakras that are most important for Fire to vitalize in the earth season are the Heart chakra and the Root chakra.

Heart chakra

To develop the inner qualities of compassion and altruism find some cornflowers or any other flowers that are strongly blue. When they have faded, sprinkle the flowers along the window-ledges in your home or beside your bed to ensure harmony and happiness for all.

If you have the chance to acquire a piece of jade, make sure it is the dark green emerald colour, known as *feits'ui* by the Chinese, or Imperial jade. This highly regarded stone can be placed on a window-ledge for seven nights (corresponding to the seven chakras) to absorb the moonlight. If you can't get hold of jade, malachite is just as powerful. However, make sure it has not been polished.

Once the stone has been cleansed by the moon, carry it round with you to warm your heart chakra with generosity and compassion.

Root chakra

The Root chakra is where our grounded energy is created. When we are in a Fire phase we may be more likely to choose spontaneity over caution, daring over prudence. The awakening of sensuality and the calmer experiences that are associated with the Root chakra can be achieved by placing rose petals under your pillow at night for self-nurturing and receptivity. To emphasize your seductive qualities and to reveal that your chakras are more than skin deep, add a few grains of dill seed to your bath-water before any intimate liaison and you will become irresistibly attractive. As Fire you may believe yourself to be the most passionate animal of the jungle, but if your Root chakra is dormant you'll never find that true intoxicating warmth of sensuality.

To ensure you achieve a more grounded basis from which to make decisions and to honour your own needs, place a moonstone in the most frequently used room of the house, touching it each time you pass by. The moonstone has the ability to direct you to the possible outcome of future choices; it gives you time to ground your impulses rather than acting upon them too hastily.

The moonstone allows your Root chakra energy to flow with more awareness, something Fire's headstrong qualities often make difficult. With your Root chakra unblocked, you may find that your body becomes more sensually aware than constantly active.

Autumn

For Fire, autumn is the time to emphasize your beauty, reflecting this in your home and surroundings. This doesn't mean that you have to redecorate the whole place, but by introducing some important Feng Shui principles into your home, you can start to balance the inner you with the outer world.

Whether you are a Fire birth element or merely going through a Fire phase, bright, stunning colours – reds or bold, shiny hues – are essential in your environment. However, it is also essential to incorporate Wood or Earth colours to balance your excessive energy levels. Natural colours ground your powerful drive. Choose one of the Wood colours for your kitchen – herby greens, wild sage, cool peppermints, forest greens or the soft pinky hues of the early morning sky. Earth colours include pistachio, gentle tones evocative of corn and spring meadows, mellow ochres and warm chestnuts and the colours you find in autumn leaves. These can be as dark as coal or as baked as terracotta. Use them to paint walls, or bring the colours into your decoration and furnishings.

To reflect your growing inner beauty, hang a painting or photograph of trees or a stunning landscape in your bedroom or bathroom. Wood remedies are useful reminders that others may not share Fire's urgency in their lifestyles. With the grace and sophistication of Wood you can blend such qualities with your more dominant traits. Earth is to ground you, Wood to expand your heart and mind!

Wood and Earth enhancements and balancers are easy to incorporate in the home: for example, arrange shells or a collection of stones or loofahs and sponges in the bathroom. In the kitchen, old glass jars filled with exotic spices like cinnamon sticks and coriander seeds will achieve the same level of energy. And if you have access to one, place a piece of smoky quartz in the hallway to improve your serenity and affection for others.

Winter

Winter is the season to work with self-empowerment for inner harmony. This is a difficult time of year for Fire. Here you are in the element of Water, where you may feel that your normal lively spirit and impatient lifestyle have been sucked into a wet and dismal hole. Water is your natural opposite, and you may find you become insufferably dominating and pushy, or just take too many risks to avoid what you feel is the draining dreariness of the dark. This is the reflective phase of the moon, a period when she hides for a while, waiting to be reborn.

The winter solstice heralds this time of the year (it is usually around 22 December), and although festive fun and the crackle of log fires can warm you and bring a touch of Fire's vanity to life again, you may also need to do some work with crystals to balance and revitalize your zest for life. Now is the time that you need to draw on all the elemental energies for self-empowerment.

Diagram 7 illustrates a Fire elemental empowerment circle. Empowerment circles protect, inspire and nurture. If you lay out an empowerment circle during the most difficult energy time of the year, you can

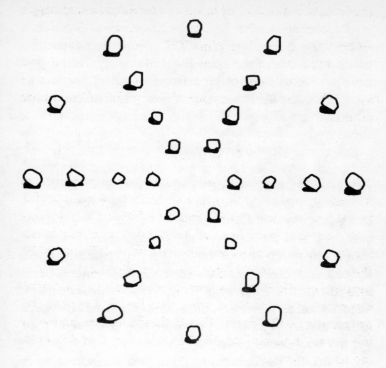

Diagram 7
Fire's dream stone empowerment circle

reflect on your own qualities, as well as combining them with those of the other elements. Thus, what was once an inauspicious period becomes a more beneficial time of year for planning and decision-making.

You can use any stones, pebbles, crystals or shells for your circle – any natural objects, in fact, as long as they are laid out in the way suggested. You may either leave the centre empty to meditate upon your dominant element or place your specific elemental talisman or crystal there as a reminder of your own worth. The natural talisman for Fire is the pine cone. The crystal for Fire is cornelian or bloodstone.

If you create the circle outside your home, make sure that it will be in the sun for at least some part of the day. Too much shade will have a depleting effect on its energy. If you create the circle inside your home, try to put it in a south-facing room (south is Fire's auspicious direction, especially in the winter).

Keep the empowerment circle intact for most of the winter, or until you feel spring is just around the corner. If you are aware of the changing phases of the moon, so much the better. At the full moon place a lighted red candle beside your empowerment circle and affirm the following: 'I am passionate and have vision; I am as vibrant as the summer sun and as warm as the golden light of the evening sky. My Fire blazes, yet my soul seeks peace.'

Once the daylight starts to linger or the spring equinox is near, you can safely clear away your empowerment stones or crystals. But keep them in a safe place (in a box or wrapped in silk) until the following winter. They are now your inner nourishers and must be respected as such.

Spring

For Fire the first blades of new grass and the smell of the sun warming the morning light signify a rush towards the summer and renewed energy. After the dormant winter and rekindling of your inner energy reserves, it's time to go out and freshen up your act for the joy of summer ahead!

Working with your appearance is now a top priority. The seeds of your inner beauty have been sown and it's time to go out and play, expanding your daring optimism into clothes, feasts, colours and fun. Use this valuable time of year, when symbolically the waxing moon is growing in strength and beauty itself, to reflect upon your clothes, fashion accessories, colour and outer style. Here are some ideas for the complete Fire style.

To enhance and emphasize your impulsive spirit, choose colours that flame, from Indian reds to smoking-jacket crimson, through to blood-orange hues. Before you go out to parties or social events, make sure that you wallow in a bath of sandalwood or spicy exotic bath oil to add Earthy sensuality to your fiery energy. Silk is a must, whether you're male or female, as it sensitizes your body.

Use your magical talisman, the pine cone, to perform the following ritual for increased vitality and peaceful sleep. If you have disrupted sleep patterns, it will restore health to your body and give you sweet dreams. Do this at the full moon. Take the pine cone in both hands and close your eyes. Choose a quiet spot and sit cross-legged with, perhaps, a smoky quartz or rose quartz crystal in front of you for added concentration. Press your fingers against the rough surface of the cone for at least two minutes while you gaze at the crystal or concentrate on the touch of the pine cone between your hands. This is an ancient, natural way to revitalize your body. Finally, when you go to bed that night place the pine cone on the window-ledge, so that it draws on the energy of the moonlight.

The Secret Chamber

The qualities you have to offer in life and those you may need to learn and develop are the keys to successful living. We often walk blindly down the street, unaware that we perceive the world only from our own eyes. Everyone else's eyes focus on something different. Each of us focuses on a different aspect of life, which is why it is important to discover how to use our Fire energy in a positive way – to see the virtues of our element phase, but also to be aware of and recognize its defects.

Defects

If you're a Fire person you may believe you have a divine right to say and do exactly as you like, without thinking about the consequences of your actions. You may be over-assertive and use anger as your weapon. Envy and resentment may build up so quickly that you deny yourself the chance for true affection. Your independent spirit may resist any attempts at diplomacy or tolerance, you may be spiralled into audacious and ever more childlike actions. If you are pushy, people may respond negatively or drop you altogether.

Virtues

However, your extraordinary inspirational vision can be valuable if you learn to share and cooperate. By showing others how to become independent and self-assured and offering them the opportunity to express their own hidden qualities, you will begin to recognize your own talent for passion and inspiration. Once you become aware of your dynamic centre, you can begin to enjoy the connection with others, while maintaining and enjoying your free, adventurous spirit and allowing your inner child more room to play. To help curb your restless and impulsive spirit, and to channel this energy into inspirational 'listening' rather than 'speaking', make sure your bed, desk, favourite sofa, chair or view faces south, the most auspicious direction for Fire.

Chapter Four

The Palace of Earth

Crystal: smoky quartz or moonstone
Natural talisman: cloves

First, make sure you have tested whether this is currently your dominant or key element. If this is not your natural birth element, you may find that your energy changes throughout the year. If so, just move into the corresponding element palace.

The Kitchen Garden is for outer and inner beauty, your body, fitness, environment and empowerment for success and self-worth. It contains Feng Shui ways to enhance your home, including rituals, moon and chakra cycles, symbols and magical affirmations and empowerments, together with auspicious times of the year for making decisions and planning.

The Secret Chamber is the place where you can

discover what you have to offer others, and what you need to learn and develop as you go through this phase.

When you walk into the Palace of Earth you are beginning a journey where the senses are awakened, where the sights, smells and sounds of the Earth season fill you with warmth and peace to nourish and harmonize your body, mind and spirit. If you are in an Earth elemental phase or true to your birth element, then you need to create and maintain grounded harmony, whether in a Dark Earth phase or a Light Earth phase.

The Kitchen Garden

Your physical appearance and well-being are simply outer manifestations of how you feel inside, emotionally, mentally and spiritually. Working with all three at once is not easy, and you may find that it is best to concentrate on one type of energy at a time. When Earth is your dominant or birth element, you need to look at what it symbolizes and represents in your life, complementing and balancing this with the other elements.

Earth can benefit from incorporating all the other four elements into the environment, but especially Metal and Fire.

Fitness

Earth is suggestive of solidity and strength, and for most Earth people endurance and commitment to a cause are the best ways to harmonize Earth's incredibly powerful, latent energy.

Earth people have an abundance of physical strength. Any kind of activity that involves a sense of purpose will be enjoyable and beneficial for Earth. Gardening is a mixture of creativity and stamina, using both the sensual pleasures that you enjoy, as well as the tenacity and perseverance of Earth's superior stamina. In traditional Chinese astrology, Earth is associated with the planet Saturn. Saturn represents boundaries, great endurance and tenacity. So you could well enjoy outdoor sports such as hiking, riding or long-distance running. Pot-holing or rock-climbing may also appeal to you if you appreciate awesome surroundings, as in fact, may any activity where you can compete against yourself rather than others.

For a less involved way to keep fit, try dance and yoga or t'ai chi. All are excellent for Earth energy balance. You may also like to use your natural sense of rhythm by making music. Although not specifically a form of exercise, playing a musical instrument uses Earth's natural skills and aligns your inner balance. If you enjoy swimming, Water may be beneficial in small doses to encourage increased communication and acceptance to change.

Vitalizing the inner you during the Fivefold Year

To complement and balance high Earth energy levels, Fire and Metal remedies can be incorporated to beautify and strengthen your inner and outer body.

The Chinese have five seasons of the year, unlike our four. They are spring, summer, Earth season,

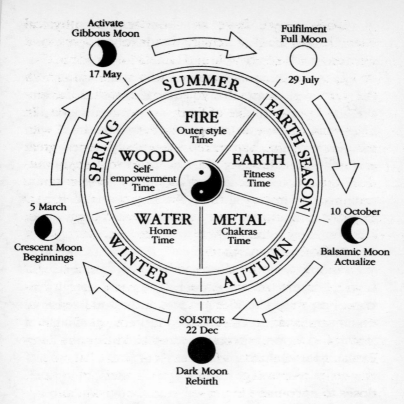

Activate
Gibbous Moon

17 May

Fulfilment
Full Moon

29 July

SUMMER

SPRING

EARTH SEASON

FIRE
Outer style
Time

WOOD
Self-
empowerment
Time

EARTH
Fitness
Time

5 March

Crescent Moon
Beginnings

WATER
Home
Time

METAL
Chakras
Time

10 October

Balsamic Moon
Actualize

WINTER

AUTUMN

SOLSTICE
22 Dec

Dark Moon
Rebirth

Diagram 8
The Fivefold Year for Earth

autumn and winter. Diagram 8 shows you how this relates to the five elements but to Earth in particular.

As you can see, the Earth season is the most auspicious season of the year for Earth. This is a time when you are in natural harmony with your environment, and symbolically the moon has just passed its highest point in the sky. It has grown and learned from experience, and, like Earth people, can begin to express and share its wisdom with full purpose and meaning.

In the Chinese Fivefold Year the summer is divided into summer and the Earth season, and crosses over into our spring and autumn. As the change from one season to another varies from year to year, use the dates on the diagram only as rough guides. For example, if you don't feel that spring has truly arrived on 5 March, don't suddenly start doing spring work until you 'feel' the time is right. It may vary by another few days, or even a week, on either side of these dates.

Each season marks a specific time for attending to your body, your environment or your inner well-being. Use the following calendar to help you. By incorporating most specifically Fire and Metal Feng Shui enhancements and employing a more cautious use of Water and Wood aspects, you can balance your Earth element for each auspicious season.

Earth season	Work with outer beauty, body fitness and food
Autumn	Time to work with chakras for inner harmony
Winter	Concentrate on your environment at home
Spring	Best time for working on self-empowerment
Summer	Work on outer style and inner feasts

Earth season

At this time of year the longest day has passed by and autumn and the smells of harvesting are beginning to fill our noses. If you live in the city you may not notice the subtle shift from summer to the Earth season, but as an Earth element it is vital that you open your awareness to discover the magic of this time of year. If you can, go out into the fields, meadows or hills and sit for a while in solitude. Although Earth people are generally well grounded, they often need to allow the Earth itself to nourish them directly. If you cannot get into open countryside, then a park, a garden or a patch of grass will do. But *smell* the grass, *touch* the blades and *feel* the movement of life across your fingers. If you manage to get out into the country, do the same thing and touch any plants or trees that you feel especially drawn to.

To ensure your outer beauty is in harmony with your own elemental season, make use of Fire elemental herbs in your cooking and in your bathroom. Pick some marigolds, or find a good herbalist or health food shop that stocks dried marigold petals. Sprinkle these in all four corners of your home. Start in the north corner, moving to the east, then to the south and lastly the west. Marigolds are renowned for their healing qualities, and by using this ritual you can free your Earth energy from its sometimes rather static nature, allowing more fantasy, provocation and daring into your life. Marigolds are also regenerators. Trading tired, worn-out patterns of living for rejuvenation and a carefree spirit is not to be scoffed at. Earth people are good at healing others, but do not often attend much to themselves for fear of change. This is why both Fire and Metal remedies can do wonders for the boundless energy trapped within a beautiful Earth person.

Olives have long been renowned for their many medicinal and healing properties. But for Earth they are without doubt a wonderful natural food that promotes the integrity and self-confidence they sometimes lack. Green and black olives are equally beneficial. Place a glass bowl of olive stones, washed and dried in the sun for a few hours, beside your bed to enhance positive thinking and inspirational dreams. Earth can often be pessimistic about the future and yet refuse to consider change as a means to success! Yet what Earth fears most is insecurity. By allowing more flexible qualities to surface, you may find that your fears become your purpose. To maintain your sensuality and seductive qualities, use sandalwood oil or essence in your bath, and to enliven your outer beauty, cast the following spell. Before you bathe, light a white candle to symbolize distinction and self-respect. As you lie back in the bath-water, sprinkle a few pinches of nutmeg on the flame. Enjoy the vapour, enhancing your outer beauty with a new inner sense of passion and daring.

To balance and energize your metabolism and digestive system, again use olives in your favourite feasts, or incorporate red chillis in a bottle of olive oil for added zest and as a gentle tonic for internal organs.

Earth season ritual

Designed to enhance your charm, sensuality and creativity for the rest of the year, this ritual is best performed near the equinox (around 22 September).

Earth needs Fire to enrich the soil, and to enliven and produce more fertile ground. Similarly, when your dominant element is Earth, you also need the spirited optimism and carefree attitude of Fire to ignite your deeper desires and enhance your outer appearance. Earth phase people are sometimes over-cautious at the expense of enjoying new experiences and just letting life happen to them. This ritual will stimulate all your senses, so that your outer world becomes more dynamic and inspiring than ever before. It will also enrich your creative urge and give you confidence in your ability to attract and enjoy a passionate lifestyle.

If you can perform this ritual outside, so much the better. Choose an evening when the moon is nearly full and there is a gentle breeze. First, find a pewter or metal goblet or cup (a tin can will do as a last resort) and a gold coin, ring or other piece of jewellery. These represent Metal magic. Place them in the centre of a special circular area you have marked out with stones or pebbles. This is your Earth totem. Now find the following plants (use either the petals or the leaves): marjoram, rose petals, magnolia leaves, apple-blossom or apple tree leaves and lavender. Don't worry if you can't find some of them, just gather those you can. Do not dry them, but sprinkle them into the metal goblet.

Next, find two scented candles (musk or sandalwood fragrance) and light them. If you prefer, use two white candles and sprinkle clove oil onto the wick so that your own natural talisman resonates with the burning wax. This is your own Earth energy, which must be offered up to the energy of Metal and Fire to balance your beauty within. As you watch the candles flicker in the breeze, affirm to yourself: 'I am of Earth, of nature's heart and of nature's desire am I her child. What treasure are these stones I cast before me, like gemstones of my inner warmth they offer serenity in a coat of passion; my enflamed heart is eager now for more.'

Autumn

When the light begins to leave our daytime early, and we see the fading sunset washed with pinks not reds or orange, then is the time for Earth to concentrate on chakra energy.

This is the time of year when symbolically the moon is waning. It is sometime called a balsamic moon, a time when one must re-evaluate what has been set down in the past, and make transformations accordingly. This is the season of Metal, and for Earth a most auspicious and sensitive time, when ambition and the instigation of any chosen pathway can unfold beneficially.

Chakra is the Sanskrit word for 'wheel'. These wheels are energy centres located at seven invisible points extending from the base of your spine to the top of your head. These spirals of invisible energy vibrate and resonate to many other energies, corresponding and relating to all aspects of our lives. By working with each chakra in turn, you can awaken yourself to more positive energy. For beauty and harmony, you need to work on sensuality and charisma. When you are in an Earth phase or you feel a deep connection to Earth or it is your birth element, you need to work especially with the chakras that correspond to Metal and Fire (see Diagram 6, page 82).

Here is a description of the chakra energy associations at their most simplified level:

Element Earth   (Root chakra) – grounded, centred, waiting, acceptance

Element Water   (Sacral chakra) – receptive, creative, sensitive, sexual

Element Fire   (Solar Plexus chakra) – vitality, vision, enthusiasm, optimism

Element Wood   (Heart chakra) – detached love, compassion, ideals, altruism

Element Metal   (Throat chakra) – power, truth, trust, responsibility

The two other chakras are the Brow chakra (psychic, intuition, insight, spirit) and the Crown chakra (cosmic consciousness, soul, threshold). However, they are not associated with the Chinese elements.

We have to work with the five elemental chakras. These five correspond to our conscious knowledge, a self-awareness we must assimilate before we can move up to the higher chakras of the Brow and the Crown. These two bring us closer to an awareness of the unconscious and beyond.

The two chakras that are most important for Earth to vitalize in the autumn season are the Solar Plexus chakra and the Throat chakra.

Five other chakras have been 'discovered' more recently, but for the purposes of our elemental journey we do not need to delve further into this highly regarded system of self-understanding, growth and healing.

Solar Plexus chakra

To ensure inner harmony for your Solar Plexus chakra place either a piece of yellow citrine or topaz on a south-west or north-east facing window-ledge in your home. Keep it there until the end of autumn. If you can't acquire even small pieces of these crystals, use the following ritual to restore inner vitality and enliven the Solar Plexus chakra.

Gather either scented geranium flowers or dandelions, but make sure the dandelions are still in flower before the seeds appear. Leave them on a window-ledge for seven nights, where they can draw in the energy of the moonlight. Then gather the petals or flower-heads into a small purse or bag made of silk or cotton, and carry it around with you for added enthusiasm and enjoyment for the future. This also aids better assimilation of the digestive system.

Throat chakra

Unblocking the Throat chakra ensures the free communication of trust and responsibility. When we are in a dominant Earth phase we find it difficult to accept anybody else's truth, relying solely on ourselves. We may stay behind closed doors to avoid taking responsibility for anything that requires more effort in our lives. Rigid and dogmatic, we may assume we know best and that we are right. This can lead to tight skin, tight lips, tight sensations and glandular problems.

To release those hidden qualities of communication and the acceptance of others' values, place a piece of white quartz or amethyst in your favourite room. Every time you pass this crystal, touch it as a reminder that you can communicate with passion and logic as well as with conviction. Opening your throat is literally allowing the words to flow! But also remind yourself that good communication is about listening, not just about speaking. Open your ears to others and their truths, for there are many consequences of one truth.

By allowing communication into your life, your inner beauty can begin to work in harmony with your outer one. Use patchouli oil in your bath whenever you feel uncertain about moving out of your caution zone, as this will help stimulate you to better self-expression.

Winter

For Earth, winter is the time to emphasize your beauty, reflecting this in your home and surroundings. This dosen't mean you have to redecorate the whole place, but by introducing some important Feng Shui principles into your home, you can start to balance the inner you with the outer world.

Winter is a time when your resonance to the seasons is at its lowest. The element of Water dominates the winter darkness, and you may feel that Water people are trying hard to prise open your habit-bound thoughts and fill them instead with fluidity and dreams. Yet, in small quantities, Water people can inspire you to communicate and express yourself more freely. Use this time of year to consolidate your growing awareness of flexibility and the ability to change.

You may feel depressed and under the weather, so make time before spring to reorganize your home and bring harmony into your environment. By incorporating Fire and Metal enhancements, you may be able to instil more zest and self-confidence into your everyday living.

Avoid too much Water or Wood. In other words, don't have a multitude of plants around your home! Because you need to express rather than absorb your close connection to the natural world, the harmony of Wood is better channelled through working with plants or animals, gardening, growing vegetables, helping reclaim woods and hedges, or just getting out into the countryside if you live in town.

Introduce white candles and gilt-edged mirrors into your environment; also Metal lighting, art deco style or even four-poster or brass bedsteads! Gilt or bronze-effect chandeliers or candelabras are excellent for improving your sense of inner worth. And try investing in antiques, or else bric-à-brac that inspires your talent for history and natural inclination for works of art. To reflect your growing inner beauty bring a painting, photograph or poster of fantastic beasts, mythological beings or passionate and erotic love scenes into your bedroom.

Metal and Fire are essential reminders that you can be as erotic and dynamic as anyone else, and get away with it. Fire is there to vitalize you, Metal to bring integrity and trust to your heart and soul. Introduce other Metal and Fire balancers and enhancers into your home: for example, their corresponding colours. Indian reds, brilliant whites, crimson, tangerine and primrose yellow, plus gold leaf or gold-painted furniture. Decorate your bathroom with gold stars and luxurious tapestries or damasks faded with age and rich in history. An instant Fire enhancer is to hang a string of dried red chilli peppers on the back of your kitchen door. Provocation can be fun!

Spring

This is the time of the year, symbolically, when the moon comes out from behind her dark cloak of mystery in the depths of silence, stirring again, emerging and initiating as her light becomes crescent and ready

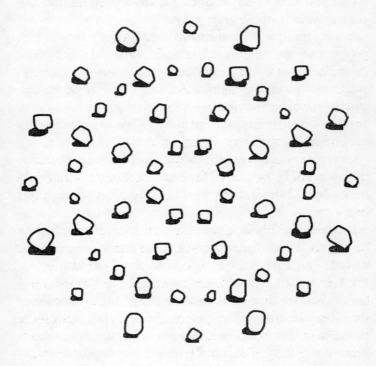

Diagram 9
Earth's centred stone empowerment circle.

to focus on the future. For Earth this is the time to work with self-empowerment for inner peace and serenity. Wood rules the springtime and is not your greatest elemental compatibility. Wood can often deplete and exhaust Earth's determination for self-reliance, preferring instead that everyone be equal and rely on one another.

Harness the power of an Earth element empowerment circle to strengthen your (see Diagram 9). However, you need to draw on *all* the elemental energies in the following way. Empowerment circles protect, inspire and nurture. By laying out an empowerment circle during the most difficult energy time of the year, you can reflect on your own qualities, as well as combining them with those of the other elements. Thus, what was once an inauspicious period becomes a more beneficial time of year for planning and decision-making.

You can use any stones, pebbles, crystals or shells for your circle – in fact, any natural objects, as long as they are laid out in the way suggested. You may either leave the centre empty to meditate upon your dominant element or place your specific elemental talisman or crystal there as a reminder of your own worth. The natural talisman for Earth is a clove. The crystal for Earth is smoky quartz or moonstone.

If you lay this circle outside your home, make sure that it will be in the sun for at least some part of the day. Too much shade will have a depleting effect upon its energy. If you create the circle inside your home, put it in a south-west or north-east facing room. These are Earth's most auspicious directions.

Maintain the circle for most of the spring, or until

you feel that summer is just around the corner. Be flexible (not easy for Earth) with the change of the season; it might not correspond to the date I have suggested. Work with your own innate sense of change, that inner quality you are becoming more and more aware of! If you are aware of the changing phases of the moon, so much the better. At the full moon, or an evening when the sky is clear, place a lighted white candle in your empowerment circle and affirm the following: 'My patience and my affection are as grounded as the path before me; the Earth spirit within me nurtures and brings gradually changing awareness. Clarity and joy can now be mine.'

Once the spring begins to turn to summer and you can really feel and smell the change in the air and see the different light, you may safely clear away your empowerment stones or crystals. But keep them in a safe place (wrap them in silk or place them in a special box) until the following spring. They are now your inner guides and must be respected as such.

Summer

This is the time for activating your new-found inner energy. With pure enjoyment you can work on your outer appearance, making it your top priority for this lively and dynamic season. Now the moon is symbolically almost full, you are ready to analyse and define who you are and what your purpose is, before stepping out into the full light of your own season. Your inner beauty has been established and it is now time to treasure your sensuality and your inner emotions and to enjoy feasts with colours, clothes and your outer style. Here are some ideas for revitalizing the complete Earth style.

The staid quality you sometimes convey outweighs your more seductive and sensual nature. To enhance and vitalize this hidden quality, wear earthy colours to maximize your appeal. Incorporate colours such as terracotta, yellow ochre, honey and burnt sienna, either as clothes or just as accessories. Rich chenilles are uncomfortably warm in summer, so go for heady perfumes or fragrances that reflect similar exotic qualities. Use patchouli oil and white musk in the bath or on your body to revitalize your skin. Silver jewellery will spice up your introspective air and lend you more single-minded determination.

Find your magical talisman – a jar of cloves is all you need – and perform the following ritual for increased vitality and peaceful sleep. This beneficial ritual is especially useful if you have difficult sleep patterns, dreams or find waking up a struggle. Pound one or two cloves in a pestle and mortar (alternatively use the end of a spoon) until reasonably well crushed. Take a small paintbrush. Mix in a little water until you have formed a thick paste. Next, find a small mirror, preferably one with eight sides (if not, a handbag mirror that you can carry around with you will do). (This little ritual should ensure that you are nourished and warmed by the energy of Fire contacting your own elemental talisman. The mirror represents Fire, the cloves Earth.)

Choose a time of day when you are feeling centred. With either your finger or the paintbrush, carefully copy and paint your Earth talisman on the surface of the mirror. Hold it before your face for some minutes while it dries, then carefully wrap it in paper and keep it on your person for the rest of the day. At night, place it beneath your pillow or under your mattress for sleep-time beauty. This also brings inner peace to restore and vitalize your outer appearance. With the season's work now complete, you can relax, calming and re-generating your grounded energy by massaging your feet with lavender oil.

The Secret Chamber

The qualities you have to offer in life and those you may need to learn and develop are the keys to successful living. Earth subjects often walk blindly down the street, unaware that what they perceive before them is seen only from their eyes. This is why they judge, criticize and comment, often unaware that they are doing so. Each of us focuses on a different aspect of life, which is why it's important to discover how to use your Earth energy in a positive way – to see the virtues of our element, but also to be aware of and recognize its defects.

Defects

If you're an Earth person you may become rigid, sticking to opinions that have no justification. Your stubborn nature can seem like pure awkwardness for the sake of it, and others may see you as self-indulgent, jealous and over-possessive. You may become obsessed with security, safety and your inner sanctuary and allow close to you only those people who present no threat to your daily routine. You may at times refuse to budge on any issue, fearing change will take you into deep waters, where you will feel vulnerable and easily manipulated by those who have more power on their side. What you need to learn is to take a chance sometimes, to be more spontaneous and enjoy your ability to seduce, but with passion rather than a begrudgingly cautious attitude.

Virtues

By showing others that their values and needs count as much as anyone else's, you can begin to establish better relationships. By opening up to the joy and experience of just existing in the here and now, you have much to offer those who search for self-reliance and self-capability. Yours is an element that trusts in nature and the gentle turn of the seasons, not in the imposed changes of society or individuals. By becoming more receptive to these outer rhythms of life, you too can honour and find peace in the self-expression and communication that you truly seek. To help energize your inner warmth, ensure your bed, desk, favourite sofa, chair or view faces south-west or north-east, two auspicious directions for Earth.

Chapter Five

The Palace of Metal

Crystal: white quartz or diamond
Natural talisman: olive

First, make sure you have tested whether this is currently your dominant or key element. If it is not your birth element, you may find that your energy changes throughout the year. If so, just move into the corresponding element palace.

The Kitchen Garden is for outer and inner beauty, your body, fitness, environment and empowerment for success and self-worth. It includes Feng Shui ways to enhance your home, including rituals, moon and chakra cycles, symbols and magical affirmations and empowerments, together with auspicious times of the year for making decisions and planning.

The Secret Chamber is the place where you can

discover what you have to offer others, and what you need to learn and develop as you go through this phase.

When you turn the key and unlock the doorway to the Palace of Metal, you are beginning a journey where you will find seasonal herbs, potent spices, fragrances, sensual oils and crystals that will nourish your body, spirit and mind. When you are in a Metal elemental phase, you need to find out how to create harmony and maintain your vitality and well-being throughout the year, whether you are in a Dark Metal phase or a Light Metal phase.

The Kitchen Garden

Your physical appearance and well-being are simply outward manifestations of how you feel inside, emotionally, mentally and spiritually. Working with all three at once is not easy and you may find that it is best to concentrate on one type of energy at a time. When Metal is your dominant or birth element you need to look at what it symbolizes and represents in your life, complementing and balancing this with the other elements. Metal can benefit from incorporating all the other four elements into the environment, but especially Earth and Water.

Fitness

Metal is a conductor of heat and energy. In the natural world Metal forms a solid and rigid state, yet it can be flexible. By its very nature Metal needs to unbend whenever possible. It stores up so much energy that

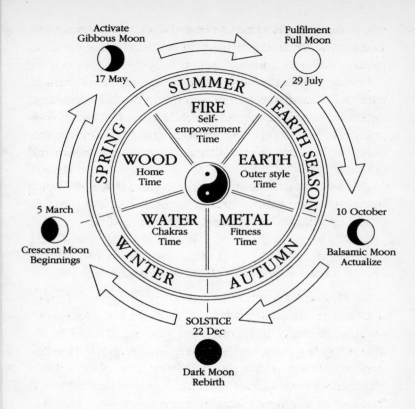

Activate
Gibbous Moon

17 May

Fulfilment
Full Moon

29 July

SUMMER

FIRE
Self-
empowerment
Time

SPRING

WOOD
Home
Time

EARTH
Outer style
Time

EARTH SEASON

5 March

WATER
Chakras
Time

METAL
Fitness
Time

10 October

Crescent Moon
Beginnings

WINTER

AUTUMN

Balsamic Moon
Actualize

SOLSTICE
22 Dec

Dark Moon
Rebirth

Diagram 10
The Fivefold Year for Metal

sudden bursts and extremes of exercise are often the only way Metal can find harmony.

Metal people need to burn up this excessive energy. Developing a sense of inner well-being may mean using such crafted sports such as t'ai chi, yoga or kitaiso. Metal people prefer self-competition rather than facing others on a racetrack or across a tennis court. You could find much enjoyment from battling against the natural elements, as in yachting (this would also bring Water into your environment, which is highly beneficial for Metal energy) or long-distance swimming. Your stamina and will are so strong that you need tough assignments at all times, especially where your body's fitness is concerned. You might find weight-training and aerobic exercise as a weekly routine improves your system and your mind.

Metal is not fond of team or social sports, but if you can take a long hike or walk and enjoy the solitude, or perhaps use your strength and skill to redesign your garden, your energy levels will be revitalized. Getting out and doing is the most important thing for Metal. Your powers of regeneration are superior to anyone else's, so use your deep reserves of energy and put them to good purpose.

Vitalizing the inner you during the Fivefold Year

To complement and balance high Metal energy levels, Earth and Water remedies can be incorporated to beautify and strengthen your inner and outer body.

The Chinese have five seasons of the year, unlike our four. These are, spring, summer, Earth season, autumn and winter. Diagram 10 shows you how this relates to the five elements and to Metal in particular.

As you can see, autumn is the most auspicious time of year for Metal. This is a time for re-evaluation and transformation, a time when Metal knows that the fullness of the year must change and decay. Nuts must be stored and gathered for the winter. This is a time to

114

actualize and prepare. Symbolically the moon is in its last quarter, and is waning, drawing in all its knowledge of the cycle to regenerate a new cycle of seasons. In the Chinese Fivefold Year summer is divided into summer and the Earth season, and crosses over into our spring and autumn. As the change from one season to another varies from year to year, use the dates on the diagram only as rough guides. For example, if you don't feel that autumn actually starts around 10 October, wait until you feel the season has changed and the time is right for you to do your autumn work. It may vary by another few days, or even a week, on either side of these dates.

Each season marks a specific time for attending to your body, your environment or your inner well-being. Below is a calendar of the seasons that are in harmony with your element for different enhancements. By incorporating most specifically Water and Earth, and employing a more careful use of Wood and Fire aspects, you can balance your Metal element for each auspicious season.

Autumn	Work with outer beauty, body, fitness and food
Winter	Time to work with chakras for inner harmony
Spring	Concentrate on your environment at home
Summer	Best time for working on self-empowerment
Earth season	Work on outer style and inner feasts

Autumn

This is the most auspicious time to work with your outer beauty, your fitness and your inner beauty combined. To ensure your outer beauty is in harmony with the autumn, gather some dried marjoram, or, if you are lucky enough to have it growing in your garden, pick some leaves and either dry them yourself in the oven or hang them in a sunny window for three days. If you use the oven method, just lay the leaves on a baking sheet for five minutes in a very hot oven. The aroma is wonderful.

Marjoram is associated with the element Earth. For Metal people Earth energy will help ground them and bring more tolerance of others into their lives. For outer beauty it can add sparkle and clarity to their appearance. Find a terracotta or china pot. This, too, is symbolic of Earth energy. Fill it with the marjoram, and then place it on a window-ledge or a place that will benefit from the moon for three nights. After this time, use the marjoram in your cooking for inner health and nourishment. Marjoram can be added to many kinds of dishes, including pasta, casseroles and salads. Anything can benefit from its delightful smell, but you most of all. Scatter a tiny pinch of the marjoram in each corner of every room of your house. This will help to revitalize and restore your charisma, attracting those whom you desire, either in love or just as good companions.

Indulge in a bath sprinkled with alluring rose petals and lavender oil to stimulate your compassion and gentleness. Metal people can often withdraw and remain highly aloof, even though on the surface they might seem as gregarious as any Water person! Yet underneath they often quiver with unspoken resentment or fear. Lavender oil is particularly beneficial to soothe you into a more passive and flexible approach to social encounters. Rose geranium oil and musk-scented candles are valuable inclusions in your bathing routine. Both stimulate and maintain a sense of connection to the inner imagination, which is often lost in Metal's need to assert logic and autonomy in their lifestyle. Being laid-back does not mean letting go of self, rather it allows the hidden self access to the world!

Autumn ritual

This is a valuable ritual to ensure you success, well-being and genuine beauty for the coming year. Metal needs Water enhancements to help in communication and connection to others, and Earth balancers to enable you to become more centred and patient with those who are not as resilient as you are. When you are in a Metal phase, or closely resonating to your birth element Metal, you need to be warmed by Earth and softened by Water to ensure your outer appearance is not only distinctive and powerful but is also backed up by compassion and sensitivity.

You can perform the following ritual on the first day you consider to be autumn, but it is more auspicious to choose the last day of autumn. This is usually easier to find, as the end of autumn in our calendar corresponds to the winter solstice or, as we usually refer to it in the West, the shortest day (usually 21 or 22 December).

First, gather some petals or leaves from any or all of the following Metal energy plants: celery leaves, peppermint, caraway, lily, violas and white roses. Next, fill

117

a glass bowl with water, and sprinkle the assorted flowers and leaves onto the surface. Place the bowl carefully in the garden or somewhere outside where it can absorb the moonlight. By offering up the bowl of Metal plants to the Water magic you are symbolically giving up your own Metal beauty to Water's natural balance. Leave the bowl overnight, but during the following evening, after the sun has set, place two lighted white candles on each side of the bowl. These are your Metal totems. To complete the ritual, first sprinkle some cinnamon powder on the lighted candle flames, and then on the bowl of flowers. As you do so, affirm to yourself: 'I am of Metal, and for integrity and wisdom do I dedicate my heart. Yet with renewed awareness, serenity and compassion will I enjoy all life, cleansing and vitalizing my inner beauty; for my body is my outer keeper and as such will I honour it.'

Winter

When winter comes, Metal subjects may be able to rediscover the delights of imagination and unpredictability in their lives. This is the most beneficial time of year to concentrate on vitalizing and unblocking your inner chakra energy. Chakra is the Sanskrit word for 'wheel'. These wheels are energy centres located at seven points extending from the base of your spine up to the top of your head. These spirals of invisible energy vibrate and resonate to many other energies, corresponding and relating to all aspects of our lives. By working with each chakra in turn, you can awaken yourself to more positive energy. For beauty and harmony, you need to work on sensuality and charisma.

When you are in a Metal phase, or you feel a deep connection to Metal or it is your birth element, you need to work especially with the chakras which correspond to Earth and Water (see Diagram 6, page 82).

Here is a description of the chakra energy associations at their most simplified level:

Element Earth   (Root chakra) – grounded, centred, waiting, acceptance

Element Water   (Sacral chakra) – receptive, creative, sensitive, sexual

Element Fire   (Solar Plexus chakra) – vitality, vision, enthusiasm, optimism

Element Wood   (Heart chakra) – detached love, compassion, ideals, altruism

Element Metal   (Throat chakra) – power, truth, trust, responsibility

The two other chakras are the Brow chakra (psychic, intuition, insight, spirit) and the Crown chakra (cosmic consciousness, soul, threshold). However, they are not associated with the Chinese elements.

We have to work with the five elemental chakras. These five correspond to our conscious knowledge, a self-awareness we must assimilate before we can move up to the higher chakras of the Brow and the Crown.

Five other chakras have been 'discovered' more recently, but for the purposes of our elemental journey we do not need to delve further into this highly regarded system of self-understanding, growth and healing.

These two bring us closer to an awareness of the unconscious, and beyond.

The two chakras that are most important for Metal to visualize are the Sacral chakra and the Root chakra.

Sacral chakra

To bring harmony to your Sacral chakra and thus to vitalize your inner hidden qualities of greater communication and sensitivity, either pick lavender leaves or buy some dried lavender flowers and place them under your pillow. As you go to sleep, make a wish that your sincerity and affection towards others may be as powerful as your integrity. If you subsequently dream of anything connected to this wish, it is highly auspicious. The following night you may like to wish also for certain dreams to come true that concern your feelings and emotions.

When we are out of tune with our Sacral chakra we are often afraid to commit ourselves or open up to others on an emotional or creatively sexual level. By aligning your outer state with this inner place, you can invite acceptance of others' emotions and your own expression of fears and feelings into your life.

Root chakra

The Root chakra is the source of grounded energy. When you are in a Metal phase, you may be more single-minded and arrogant than affectionate and sensual. These hidden qualities and the pleasures associated with Root chakra harmony can be achieved by the following daily ritual.

Obtain a small jar or pot of cloves (you can also use clove oil in your bath for receptivity and sensual awareness). Hold a handful of cloves tightly in your hand and think carefully and clearly about acceptance and centredness. Then scatter the cloves across a table. Look at the pattern they create as they fall, and try to imagine what the image they make means to you. Awareness of such symbols and patterns in our lives can vitalize our own deeper responsiveness.

As a Metal person, you are aware enough to acknowledge your sexuality, but to ensure mutual acceptance and sexual receptivity and communication, place a piece of amber or aquamarine in the most used room in the house. Each time you pass it, touch it. Amber has the power to absorb selfishness and give out greater compassion and flexibility.

With your Root and Sacral chakras unblocked and enlivened, you may find your body more sensually awakened and genuinely responsive to others.

Spring

For Metal, spring is the time to invoke harmony in your environment that reflects your own inner beauty. Nurturing your home will actualize and instil more harmony into your outer well-being. This doesn't mean you have to redecorate the whole place, but by introducing some Feng Shui remedies and principles into your home you can start to balance the inner you with the outer world.

First, make sure your house is not filled with too many gold- or silver-coloured objects or colours. If you surround yourself with too much of your own element, you may stimulate an exaggeration of your Metal qualities. Although this may make you incredibly powerful and wealthy, it won't necessarily make you happy! Greed is not the same as hunger. Contentment and tranquillity are about knowing when to stop demanding more.

To harmonize and energize your inner beauty, Earth and Water enhancements will bring a greater sense of sharing and communication to your single-minded and sometimes solitary lifestyle. Using shells picked up on a beach, smooth pebbles or weathered stones and fragments of glass, place them in the bathroom or a prominent place in your bedroom. If possible, find natural stones with holes in them, that is, holes that have been made by natural changes in the Earth, or scoured out by underground water and rain. These kind of stones possess great powers, and are highly valued in many primitive societies. Any ancient pieces of rock you pick up on country walks or by the sea shore will do. If you don't have access to the sea or the country, choose an unpolished piece of amber or turquoise and place it in a west-facing window.

Place a bowl of coloured blue and black marbles on the highest surface of your favourite room. You may not be able to see the Water hues and its energy, but it will be working for you. Alternatively, hang a painting or photograph of waterfalls, a seascape or fast-flowing rivers in the bathroom. These Water remedies energize your need to express your desires and to accept that others have values that differ distinctly from your own.

Earth hues can be incorporated into your colour

scheme, such as rich ochres, terracottas and warm umbers. Thse will inspire you towards a better understanding of how you need to relate to others. Earth brings awareness of the self and others, Water of the need to connect the two by means of intuition and communication. Place a piece of smoky quartz in the hallway to improve genuine affection for those closest to you.

Summer

Time to work with self-empowerment for inner harmony. This can often be an electric time of year for Metal, as you are travelling through the Element of Fire.

Fire is not totally compatible with Metal, as it enflames and encourages it to become even more determined and dominant. An over-empowered Metal person will lock swords with others and eventually themselves.

Going through this season can feel like an electric storm, with every current in your body charged for conflict or lightning responses (leaving you feeling as if you must either become a dictator or a saint). You may become irritated by people who seem to think only of themselves, and yet you refuse to budge where your own opinions are concerned. You may find that the Fire energy emphasizes your more cynical side, and you become arrogant and inflexible when it comes to making arrangements or decisions. This is the time of the year when, symbolically, the moon is ready to become full, a time when analysis and refinement are needed for the moment of the moon's bright glow to give meaning and purpose.

Now is the time when you need to draw on all the elemental energies for self-empowerment (see Diagram 11).

Empowerment circles protect, inspire and nurture. By laying out an empowerment circle during the most difficult energy time of the year, you can reflect on your own qualities, as well combining them with those of the other elements. Thus, what was once an inauspicious period becomes a more beneficial time of year for planning and decision-making.

You can use any stones, pebbles, crystals or shells for your circle – in fact, any natural objects, as long as they are laid out in the way suggested. You may either leave the centre empty to meditate upon your dominant element, or place your specific elemental talisman or crystal there as a reminder of your own worth. The natural talisman for Metal is the olive tree (olives or their stones are equally powerful as a talisman). The crystal for Metal is white quartz or diamond.

If you arrange the circle outside your home, make sure that it will be in the sun for at least some part of the day. Too much shade will have a depleting effect upon its energy. If you create the circle inside your home, make sure it is in a west-facing room (Metal's auspicious direction). Obviously, not everyone possesses a diamond, but white quartz crystal is widely available and just as effective. If you prefer to use olives (black or green will do), take out the stones, wash them, allow them to dry off in the sun for a few days, then pile them in a small glass container and place it in the centre of your circle.

Keep the empowerment circle for most of the summer or until around 29 July, when the Earth season

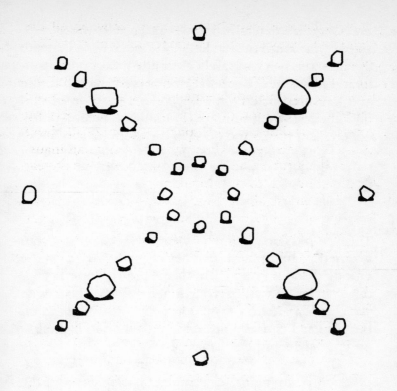

Diagram 11
Metal's cosmic stone empowerment circle

begins. If you are aware of the changing phases of the moon, so much the better. At the full moon, place a lighted white candle beside your empowerment circle and affirm the following to yourself: 'Dedication to beauty and honouring myself are my true aims. Through Metal I regenerate and transform. With purity and vision I may heal both my inner world, and the outer that encompasses all life.'

Once the days begin to shorten and the golden skies of the Earth season light the clouds from beneath the horizon, you can safely clear away your empowerment stone circle. Keep the stones or crystals in a safe and treasured place, (in a box or wrapped up in silk) until the following summer (or until you enter a different element phase and need to use them for a different season). They are now your inner nourishers, and must be respected as such.

Earth season

This is a passionate time of year for Metal, when your magnetic charm and distinctive style need to be groomed and nurtured. This is the time to look at your outer style, as well as your inner one. Working with your appearance is now a top priority. Your inner beauty has been established, so it's time to capitalize on your style and charismatic looks.

The moon is symbolically beginning to wane. Expression of opinions, dissemination of ideas and the sharing of responsibility become issues, and your outer style reflects your inner self. Here are some ideas for the complete Metal style.

You have vision and integrity and can really make an impact when you choose. With such a powerful presence, those around you have little choice but to notice you. Often you may be the most distinctive and stylishly dressed person in your circle. To enhance your eroticism, wear dark, sensual colours and a sapphire or a piece of lapis lazuli. Gold strings, jewellery or watches will magnetize and attract, while oriental oils and musky perfumes are excellent for asserting your

126

individuality. As for colours, choose white, black or rich dark blues and violets. And to vitalize your skin, hair, body and general well-being, make use of the following ritual.

Cast a circle of herbs around you, so that you are standing in the centre. Use dill seeds, marjoram, lavender, clover and rosemary. You can either use dried or fresh leaves or flowers, but make sure the circle is unbroken. Now take your natural crystal, and sit cross-legged in your circle. Hold the crystal tightly in your hands for one minute. Remove the herbs and place them in a special paper bag or, if they need drying, lay them in the sun, then collect and keep them in an airtight tin or container.

When you go to bed place the crystal on a window-ledge where it can draw on the energy of the moonlight. Your body and appearance will soon be revitalized and glowing.

The Secret Chamber

The qualities you have to offer in life and those you may need to learn and develop are the keys to successful living. Metal people often walk blindly down the street, unaware that what they perceive before them is seen only from their eyes. This is why they judge, criticize and comment, often unaware that they are doing so. Each of us focuses on a different aspect of life, which is why it's important to discover how to use your Metal energy in a positive way – to see the virtues of your element, but also to be aware and recognize its defects.

Defects

If you're a Metal person you may assume control without allowing others to have their say or investment in decisions. There may be times when your extreme nature means you cut yourself off and end arrangements, deals or even relationships without a second thought for who or what is involved. Often fanatical and obsessive if your needs aren't met, you may seem threatening to many less autonomous souls. Thus, it may be difficult for you to form genuine, warm friendships or close partnerships. Many relationships may be discarded on your journey forwards. Yet you are, underneath, a lonely person, and your arrogance is only a defence mechanism. Few are as wise as you or able to understand that a hard and detached air often hides a truly vulnerable soul.

Virtues

Being Metal means you are motivated and enterprising. You have the gift to create great practical realities out of simple dreams. Your honesty, integrity and determination can be invaluable to others in the workplace or in relationships. By being autonomous you have the chance to respond openly and with great insight into the world of the human mind. Your talent for taking control in a crisis can lead you to great achievements and success. But you must make room for communication and try to articulate your own needs.

By acknowledging the difference in each and every individual, you can bring balance and harmony to your own life, no longer distorted by judgements or the need for perfection. Your discernment is an invaluable source of inspiration to others to get to really know themselves, and you may experience the joy of transforming other people's lives, introducing them to self-mastery and self-control. To help channel this energy, make sure your bed, desk, favourite chair or sofa faces west, the most auspicious direction for Metal.

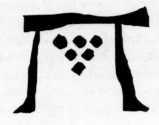

Chapter Six

The Palace of Water

Crystal: amber or turquoise
Natural talisman: four-leaved clover

First, make sure you have tested whether this is currently your dominant or key element. If it is not your natural birth element, you may find that your energy changes throughout the year. If so, just move into the corresponding element palace. The Kitchen Garden is for outer and inner beauty, your body, fitness, environment and empowerment for success and self-worth. It contains Feng Shui ways to enhance your home, including rituals, moon and chakra cycles, symbols and magical affirmations and empowerments, together with auspicious times of the year for making decisions and planning. The Secret Chamber is the place where you can discover what you have to offer others, and what you may need to learn and develop as you go through this phase.

Here in the Palace of Water you will meet the sensitive draw of the ocean currents, the fluid and ever-changing nature of the seas that may revitalize and nourish your body mind and spirit. If you are in a dominant Water elemental phase, or true to your birth element, then you need to create and maintain harmony, whether in a Dark Water phase or a Light Water phase.

The Kitchen Garden

Your physical appearance and well-being are simply outer manifestations of how you feel inside, emotionally, mentally and spiritually. Working with all three of these at once is not easy and you may find that it is best to concentrate on one type of energy at a time. When Water is your dominant or birth element, you need to look at what it symbolizes and represents in your life, complementing and balancing this with the other elements. Water can benefit from incorporating all the other four elements into the environment, but especially Wood and Metal.

Fitness

In view of the gregarious and scattered nature of Water energy, you may find attending to your fitness is a chore rather than an enjoyable expression of your bodily needs. Water people are highly sensitive to those around them and find they transmit and receive all kinds of energies when in large crowds or busy environments. Team sports and highly energetic, busy activities are not suited to your gentle and psychic nature. You may find swimming, cruising in boats and other water activities are the best ways of keeping fit. You would also do well to look to solitary games such as golf, brisk country walks or disciplines like yoga and t'ai chi to restore your bodily balance. The planet Mercury is associated with Water in Chinese astrology. Mercury is about dexterity, speed and highly charged nervous energy, so you may do well in sports such as tennis, archery, darts, fencing or anything that requires a quick mind and nimble feet or fingers. Long-distance running or endurance tests of strength are not for you!

Your unpredictable nature could mean that you change your form of fitness regularly; for example, signing up at the local aerobics class, only to decide to go for a yachting course instead. Whatever it is that motivates you to enjoy physical exercise, follow that particular pathway. Being elusive and transient, all kinds of stimulation appeal to you. Dance, music and singing can restore your inner balance without you having to perform for the outside world. This may bring self-posession and more stability to your lifestyle.

Vitalizing your inner beauty during the Fivefold Year

To complement and balance high Water energy levels, Wood and Metal remedies can be incorporated to beautify and strengthen your inner and outer body.

The Chinese have five seasons of the year, unlike our four. They are spring, summer, the Earth season,

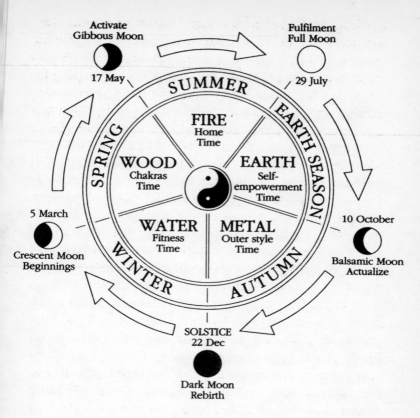

Diagram 12
The Fivefold Year for Water

autumn and winter. Diagram 12 shows you how this relates to the five elements and to Water in particular.

For Water, the most auspicious time of the year is winter. Symbolically this is when you are most in harmony with the natural rhythms of the seasons. The winter solstice marks the beginning of the winter season, usually around 22 December. The moon is

133

now symbolically in the days of the Dark Moon period, just before the New Moon. This is a time when ideas begin to germinate, when dreams are lived and the seeds of new growth are pushed into the ground, ready for rebirth and regeneration. Life lies dormant, as nature awaits the emergence and initiation of new forms, new ideas: 'If winter comes, can spring be far behind?'

In the Chinese Fivefold Year summer is divided into summer and the Earth season, and it crosses over into our spring and autumn. As the change from one season to another varies from year to year, use the dates on the diagram as rough guides only. For example, if you don't really feel that spring has arrived on 5 March, don't begin your spring work until you really feel that the time is right. This may vary by another few days, or even by a whole week, on either side of these dates.

Each season marks a specific time for attending to your body, your environment, or your inner well-being. Use the following calendar to help you. By incorporating most specifically Metal and Wood Feng Shui elements, and employing a more cautious use of Earth and Fire aspects, you can balance your Water element for each auspicious season.

Winter	Work with outer beauty, body, fitness and food
Spring	Time to work with chakras for inner harmony
Summer	Concentrate on your environment at home

| Earth season | Best time for working on self-empowerment |
| Autumn | Work on outer style and inner feasts |

Winter

Your moods may fluctuate quite dramatically during your own season. There will be times when you are extremely outgoing and sociable, then other occasions when you may withdraw and retreat into your nest, preferring solitude and sloth to company and frivolity. This inconsistency can be balanced if you use winter as your special time.

Although your flexible approach to life is one that inspires and carries you down a waterfall of spirited adventure, there are times when you need to build up the resilience and integrity of Metal and the cooperation of Wood.

If the winter makes you feel like escaping to warmer climes, then make sure you pack Wood elemental enhancements in your luggage. One of the most potent energizers for Water when travelling – and Water *is* always travelling in one way or another – is comfrey. You can usually acquire comfrey as a dried herb from the leaves or as a powder from the root. Either will be sufficient.

Place the herb or powder inside a wooden box or even a matchbox. Place the box at the bottom of your suitcase, handbag, hold-all, etc, and travel with it throughout the winter season to enhance sophistication and poise in any situation.

For greater self-confidence and dedication, use sandalwood oil in your bath, and if possible, acquire a piece of sandalwood that you can hold in your hand (you often find small figures carved out of sandalwood in oriental shops). Last thing at night, place the piece of wood under your pillow for energizing your powers of persuasion and a flexible attitude to life. While bathing, light a scented candle, preferably patchouli or white musk fragrance, and as you lounge in the sandalwood oil or foam bath, sprinkle the water with lavender or rosemary flowers to bring an exotic quality to your outer beauty. You may even find the more unfocused and impressionable side of your nature clarifies and you can begin to communicate your true feelings rather than merely reflecting other people's opinions.

To restore order to a nervous system that is often stressed out and highly charged, use olives and olive oil in your favourite meals. Also, use rosemary and thyme in your cooking pot to cleanse and purify your digestive system.

Winter season ritual

This is best performed around the winter solstice, otherwise known as the 'shortest day'. This ritual will enliven, enhance and improve your charming and seductive nature for the rest of the year, and ensure your non-commital approach to life is balanced with gentle persistence.

Water creates Wood in the natural cycle of the elements, but it draws on Metal to bring electricity and the spark of self-awareness to its fluid nature. Water people are often rushing around everywhere in a search for answers and never really finding them. This ritual may help you to focus on yourself, so that you no longer feel distracted by other people's psychic energy. This ritual can enrich your natural affinity for communication and sense of others, without leading you into fickle and neurotic patterns of behaviour. If possible, perform this ritual outside on a sharp and still winter's night. Choose an evening when there is a crescent moon if you can.

Your Metal magic or totem must include one of the following: mistletoe, gold, silver, a piece of tiger's eye, a pewter or other metal cup or goblet. For your Wood magic you need about three handfuls of the following mixture of plant flowers or leaves: rosemary, thyme, apple tree leaves, bay leaves, geranium and winter pansies. These should first have been gathered and left for one night and one day in the place where the ritual will be performed. You don't have to gather all of them, just the ones you can find. (If you find it difficult to obtain these in the winter, just use one handful of ready dried herbs.)

Place the Metal magic you have chosen on a white cloth draped over a wall, tree stump, garden chair or table — anything which is above ground level. Remember, if you do use mistletoe, make sure it never touches the ground once you have acquired the bough! This winter plant was known as the Healer of All by the Druids, and has extraordinary magical properties. It was considered extremely unlucky to place it on the ground.

Next, light two green or yellow candles and cast the handfuls of herbs across the Metal totem. This is your own Water energy, which is being offered up to the energy of Metal and Wood and will balance your inner beauty. As you do so, affirm the following to yourself either aloud or by writing it down and then burying the paper: 'Of Water am I. With flowing energy I pour creative love into others' souls. My psychic sense can now be offered freely. With warmth and understanding, with poise and dedication, shall I make music to live by.'

Spring

As the days begin to lengthen again, and symbolically the moon has begun to change from a thin sliver of the new to the crescent shape of focused growth, the time is right to work with your chakra energy. This is the time for Water to overcome the fears and inconsistencies, and to allow time for oneself, rather than devotion solely to others. This is the season of Wood, and for Water a highly auspicious time for acquiring a more detached attitude.

Chakra is the Sanskrit word for 'wheel'. These wheels are energy centres located at seven invisible points extending from the base of your spine to the top of your head. These spirals of invisible energy vibrate and resonate to many other energies, corresponding and relating to all aspects of our lives. By working with each chakra in turn, you can awaken yourself to more positive energy. For beauty and harmony, you need to work on sensuality and charisma. When you are in a Water phase or you feel a deep connection to Water or it is your birth element, you need to work especially with the chakras that correspond to Metal and Wood (see Diagram 6, page 82).

Here is a description of the chakra energy associations at their most simplified level:

Element Earth   (Root chakra) – grounded, centred, waiting, acceptance

Element Water   (Sacral chakra) – receptive, creative, sensitive, sexual

Element Fire   (Solar Plexus chakra) – vitality, vision, enthusiasm, optimism

Element Wood   (Heart chakra) – detached love, compassion, ideals, altruism

Element Metal   (Throat chakra) – power, truth, trust, responsibility

The two other chakras are the Brow chakra (psychic, intuition, insight, spirit) and the Crown chakra (cosmic consciousness, soul, threshold). We have to work with the five elemental chakras. These correspond to our conscious knowledge, a self-awareness we must assimilate before we can move up to the higher chakras of the Brow and the Crown. These two bring us closer to an awareness of the unconscious, and beyond.

The two chakras that are most important for Water are the Throat chakra and the Heart chakra.

Five other chakras have been 'discovered' more recently, but for the purposes of our elemental journey we do not need to delve further into this highly regarded system of self-understanding, growth and healing.

Heart chakra

This can be energized by placing a piece of jade or green tourmaline (which is cheaper!) on a north-facing window-ledge. Tourmaline is one of the most beautiful of stones and helps us combine the energizing quality of the universe with an enhanced sense of our own self-worth. Keep it here until the end of spring. If you can't get hold of these crystals use the following ritual to restore balance to your Heart chakra.

Once your Heart chakra is unblocked, you will find that you can love more unconditionally, and remember to care about yourself as well as others. With such a gregarious nature, you may lose touch with self-love. By arousing gentle stimulation of your Heart chakra you will start to feel compassion and tenderness – for yourself, as well as every one who comes to your door!

For this ritual, either gather seven fresh mint leaves, or seven pieces of handmade paper. Leave them on a window-ledge for seven nights, then gather the leaves (if you use paper crumple it into little balls) and place them in a small purse or fabric bag. Carry them around with you for as long as you need to feel open to others, but not vulnerable to their energy. Hang a garland of rosemary and thyme inside your front entrance above the door for a deeper acknowledgement of your own self-worth.

Throat chakra

You may need to unblock your Throat chakra, so that your inner integrity and ability to take responsibility for your actions and your feelings can be stimulated.

To help release tension in the Throat chakra, place a sandalwood carving or a piece of white quartz crystal in your bedroom.

Each morning when you rise, touch the talisman, and each night when you go to bed, hold it between your hands for three minutes while you wish for compassion and harmony for you and your relationships. By acknowledging your own self-value, and with your chakras unblocked, your outer beauty will align more freely with your inner one. To stimulate your outer beauty, use patchouli oil and/or honeysuckle oils and luxuriate in your bath.

Summer

For Water summer is the time to work with your outer beauty by creating a more harmonious environment in your home surroundings. Fire has a natural affinity with summer, and you may find that you need a certain amount of Fire in your life to stimulate your mind. Fire people, however, can drown in your watery world of elusive thoughts and actions. They like vision and purpose, while Water people love the idea of it, but have an opt-out clause from any purpose!

By incorporating Wood, Fire and Metal Feng Shui remedies, you can bring harmony into your environment in time for the Earth season, and ensure you have more self-esteem, spontaneity and enjoyment in all aspects of your life.

Wood is the most animating remedy for your home. However, we are surrounded by wooden furniture, books and papers, so make sure that you bring a special Wood enhancement into your favourite room. Try and find a wooden carving of a bird – the freedom that a bird symbolizes enables you to remain more detached when others unconsciously overwhelm you with their emotional needs. If you can't find a bird, wear a piece of carved wooden jewellery, especially if it's ebony, a perfect blend of Metal and Wood enhancement.

Place a piece of malachite or a jade ornament in a south-facing room to add panache and sophistication to your outer personality. Fire balancers to liven up your love life or working environment include white candles and sandalwood incense. Fabrics can be rich and vibrantly coloured. Try to find a painting or print of a wild, mountainous landscape and hang it on your bedroom wall above the bed. Silver must be incorporated with care as it can make Water people more sensitive than they usually are. This is because silver is associated with the moon, and the moon is a highly receptive and reflective symbol of Water's intuitive feeling.

If you have the money, include some false or real gold into your interior design, either as colour or in the form of brass and copper pots and pans in your kitchen. Metal doesn't have to be heavily invasive in your home. Perhaps you could also include a vibrant melange of fuchsia and turquoise in your colour scheme, or paint everything white and complement and contrast it with lively colours to add that fiery revitalizing sparkle!

Earth season

Now is the time when the moon is symbolically at her greatest. She is full, and loaded with passionate meaning and purpose. This can be a difficult time of year for

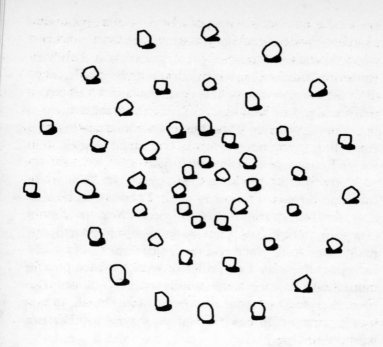

Diagram 13
Water's spiral stone empowerment circle

Water, for in Earth's elemental season you may have difficulty grounding and centring your energy, when you'd much rather be ready to take off at a moment's notice, or at least have the chance to change your mind! This is the time for you to focus and direct your powerful imagination and psychic ability. Earth can literally absorb Water and drain you of your fluidity and flexible attitude. But for self-empowerment, you need to draw on all the energies of the elements, including

Earth, by harnessing the power of a Water element empowerment circle (see Diagram 13).

Empowerment circles protect, inspire and nurture. By laying out an empowerment circle during the most difficult energy time of the year, you can reflect your own qualities as well as combining them with those of the other elements. Thus what was once an inauspicious period becomes a more beneficial time of year for planning and decision-making.

You can use any stones, pebbles, crystals or shells for your circle – in fact, any natural objects, as long as they are laid out in the way suggested. You may either leave the centre empty to meditate upon your dominant element, or place your specific elemental talisman or crystal there as a reminder of your own value. The natural talisman for Water is a four-leaved clover. The natural crystal for Water is amber or lapis lazuli. (Four-leaved clovers *do* exist, but if you would rather not waste your time hunting for one, then an image, drawing, painting or pencil sketch will do. Alternatively, you can use lavender flowers.) If you create the circle outside the house, make sure it receives sunlight for at least a few hours of the day, as too much shadow will deplete its energy. If you place it in the house, make sure it is in a north-facing room or corner, the most auspicious direction for Water.

Keep the circle until you feel the end of the Earth season has arrived. Use the date I have suggested, or if true to your Water nature, work with your own intuitive response to change. If you can view the phases of the moon, so much the better. Around the time of the full moon, place a lighted blue candle in your empowerment circle and affirm to yourself: 'My spirits flow like the waters of time. With the senses of the universe I can connect to every moment, with the hearts of every being I am made aware of my value; now is the time to prize myself.'

As soon as you feel the change of the seasons, you can safely clear away your empowerment circle. Keep the stones or crystals in a safe place (wrap them in a beautiful fabric or place in a special box) until the following Earth season, or when your elemental energy changes. These are now your inner nourisher and must be respected as such.

Autumn

To make use of your seductive qualities and charm friends and lovers, draw on your own Water beauty at this time of year to activate your inner self-worth. Treasure your beguiling and unpredictable nature. Here are a few ideas for vitalizing the complete Water style.

To enhance your seductive quality, wear soft violets, viridians or Prussian blues. Clothes should be light, ephemeral and airy, fabrics that move with you rather than pin you down and drag you to the ground! Most Water people are fast, quick on their feet and always in a rush to get on with the next experience. To calm your nervous and restless energy, wear musky perfumes, bathe in cedarwood, bergamot or rose-scented oils to quieten and still your over-active mind.

Here is a special beauty ritual to establish harmony for your over-active metabolism. Water people need to feel in touch with their inner world and may find that remembering their dreams can do wonders for their outer style and inner happiness. Make a dream pillow from chamomile flower petals. Either use a small cloth and just tie up the petals and place it under your own pillow, or lay it beside your bed where the fragrance and power of the herbs can infuse all your senses while you sleep. If you can't find chamomile petals, you can use chamomile tea instead. This dream pillow may help relieve you of the outer anxieties that Water is prone to experience.

The Secret Chamber

The qualities you have to offer in life and those you may need to learn and develop are the keys to successful living. Water subjects often walk blindly down the street unaware that what they perceive before them is seen only from their eyes. This is why they judge, criticize and comment, often unaware that they are doing so. Each of us focuses on a different aspect of life, which is why it's important to discover how to use your Water energy in a positive way – to see the virtues of your element but also to be aware of and recognize its defects.

Defects

If you're a Water person you may be inclined to look too quickly for answers, side-stepping conflict and leading others to assume you lack depth. You can appear fickle and inconsistent, interested only in being the centre of attention if you don't have to become committed. You may be so sensitive to the needs of others that you forget your own and end up being a reflection of everyone else, never knowing who you really are. Others may take advantage of your good nature, and you may begin to resent close friendships. Your vulnerability may emerge as hesitation and indecision, so that others don't know where they stand with you. Being all things to all people takes its toll on your energy levels, and you may often find yourself floundering in self-doubt and confusion, preferring to dream of possibilities rather than take realistic and practical action to obtain your goals.

Virtues

Your gifts include a real awareness of how others feel. Your sensitivity can work wonders if you allow them to realize you have feelings too. You may be an excellent listener, but you need to communicate your own needs as well. By showing you have a deep and immeasurable contact with both the spiritual and the profane, and that by feeling your way in life rather than merely using logic, you can teach others the power of intuition. You have the ability to communicate things in heaven and earth that few others have time even to consider. Your sense of relationship, both with the world around you and with individuals, is acute and accurate, honed by experience and the extraordinary encounters you have throughout your life.

Others may begin to see the value of your flexibility, and you, too, may gradually realize that your inner values are those of self-expression, creativity and transformation. Your need for change is innate, but armed with the awareness that you are able to impress and beguile others with life's mysteries rather than with life's vague imaginings, yours will be a centred and truly compassionate quest for self. To help energize your integrity, ensure your bed, desk, favourite chair or sofa or view faces north, the most auspicious direction for Water.

Chapter Seven

The Palace of Wood

Crystal: malachite, jade, green tourmaline
Natural talisman: pomegranate or apple

First, make sure you have tested whether this is currently your dominant or key element. If it is not your natural birth element, you may find that your energy changes throughout the year. If so, just move into the corresponding element palace. The Kitchen Garden is for outer and inner beauty, your body, fitness, environment and empowerment for success and self-worth. It contains Feng Shui ways to enhance your home, including rituals, moon and chakra cycles, symbols and magical affirmations and empowerments, together with auspicious times of the year for making decisions and planning. The Secret Chamber is the place where you can discover what you have to offer others, and what

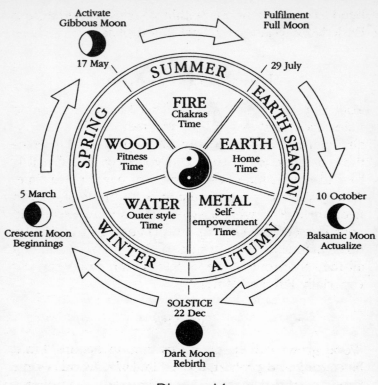

Diagram 14
The Fivefold Year for Wood

you may need to learn and develop as you go through
this phase.

As you enter the Palace of Wood you are stepping
into a place where sophistication, poise and freedom
will dictate your attitude to the rest of the world. Here,
love of mankind nourishes and revitalizes your body,
mind and soul. If you are in a dominant Wood elemental phase or are true to your birth element, then you

150

need to create harmony within your life, whether in a Dark Wood phase or a Light Wood phase.

The Kitchen Garden

Your physical appearance and well-being are simply outer manifestations of how you feel inside, emotionally, mentally and spiritually. Working with all three of these at once is not easy and you may find that it is best to concentrate on one type of energy at a time. When Water is your dominant or birth element, you need to look at what it symbolizes and represents in your life, complementing and balancing this with the other elements. Wood can benefit from incorporating all the other four elements into the environment, but especially Fire and Water.

Fitness

Wood grows slowly, taking its time to mature, but it has strong and probing roots. Similarly, Wood people need to take their time, with their eccentric energy levels. They have a powerful drive towards the future outcome of their channelled energy, and are severely self-critical if they don't live up to their own expectations.

If Wood is your birth or dominant element, you may need to pursue sports and recreation that centre on individual attainment and experimental activities. Not for you the sports field, team games or gentle keep-fit down at the gym. The great outdoors often beckons, whether parachute-jumping, white-water rafting or mountaineering. Anything that tests your appetite for the unusual, the difficult and the challenging. The more time you have to plan your strategy for physical endurance, the better the enjoyment.

In traditional Chinese astrology the planet Jupiter rules Wood people. Jupiter represents expansion, so you may be drawn to trying out new ideas and new techniques – the weirder and wackier the sport or recreation the better! Wood seeks answers, truths and wisdom, and you may find it through self-competition. Deep-sea and scuba-diving, or high-board diving and surfing all provide an unusual blend of Water and Wood that can harmonize and stimulate an unbalanced Wood person. By incorporating Fire methods, you may also find that rock-climbing, motor racing or high-speed downhill skiing provide you with a greater sense of adventure.

Vitalizing your inner beauty during the Fivefold Year

To complement and balance high Wood energy levels, Fire and Water remedies can be incorporated through rituals to beautify and strengthen your inner and outer body.

The Chinese have five seasons of the year, unlike our four. They are spring, summer, the Earth season, autumn and winter. Diagram 14 shows you how this relates to the five elements and to Wood in particular.

The best time of the year for Wood is the spring. This is the time when you are naturally in rhythm with the seasons, a time for making plans, choices, changing jobs or moving house. Wood needs room, and the season of spring gives you space to move freely, to acknowledge your responsibilities for yourself without fearing unreasonable commitment to others. – Wood's biggest problem!

In the Chinese Fivefold Year summer is divided into summer and the Earth season, and it crosses over into our spring and autumn. As the change from one season to another varies from year to year, use the dates on the diagram as rough guides only. For example, if you don't really feel that spring has arrived on 5 March, don't begin your spring work until you really feel that the time is right. It may vary by another few days, or by even a whole week, on either side of these dates.

Each season marks a specific time for attending to your body, your environment or your inner well-being. Use the following calendar to help you. By incorporating most specifically Metal and Wood Feng Shui elements, and employing a more cautious use of Earth and Fire aspects, you can balance your Water element for each auspicious season.

Spring	Work with outer beauty, body, fitness and food
Summer	Time to work with chakras for inner harmony
Earth season	Concentrate on your environment at home
Autumn	Best time for working on self-empowerment
Winter	Work on outer style and inner feasts

Spring

The changing skies and the ever-increasing light in the evenings mean Wood has more room to breathe. Wood people often live fast-paced city lives, but even those who are firmly committed to their work may need to unwind and experience the wide open spaces to really energize and bring harmony to their body, soul and mind. The Spring is the time to work with your outer and inner beauty. By using Fire and Water elemental herbs and rituals you can make sure you are constantly receptive to new and different ideas, and can perfect the schemes for the future you may have already envisaged in your mind. By instilling inner balance, your outer charisma will become sparkling and poised. Use Water and Fire elemental herbs in your cooking and when bathing.

If you live near the sea, gather seaweed. If you are in a big city you may be able to purchase seaweed imported specially for cooking. The Chinese are very fond of crispy seaweed, so go to your local Chinese restaurant and harmonize your digestive system with an occasional treat! Ground nutmeg, chillis and garlic are Fire energizers and can be incorporated in your cook pots with ease. Wood people are very experimental with their food and like to perfect every type of cuisine. These Fire enhancers will also give you extra spontaneity to help achieve your dreams, and add a positive dynamism to your sophisticated style. They also ensure your digestive system is balanced and vitalized.

For your bath use lavender oil. This opens your mind and make you more sensitive to the needs of others. Gather any of the following herbs or flowers, either petals or leaves, and mix them together in a stone vessel: lavender, meadowsweet, lily of the valley, caraway, hops, honeysuckle or geraniums. To generate romance, scatter some of these herbs across your bath before you bathe. Alternatively, light a red candle for passion and sprinkle some of the lavender flowers onto the flame. The incense will inspire and connect you to a new inner sense of excitement tinged with ardour.

Spring season ritual

Around the spring equinox, which usually falls around 20 March, perform the following ritual for increased self-awareness and to improve and focus on your ideals. This ritual will enhance your creative urge and give you confidence in your ability to attract and enjoy a passionate lifestyle. Wood people are often scared of others becoming dependent on them. Your individuality must at all costs remain intact, yet this ritual can stimulate your responsiveness, and bring others into your life who respect your ideals of freedom and non-possession.

First, gather the following plant flowers, leaves, petals or dried herbs: rosemary, thyme, apple leaves or flower buds, catmint, feverfew, garden mint, wild roses, oak leaves. You don't have to gather all of them, just the ones you can find. These should be crushed (but don't use a metal utensil to do this as Metal is degenerative to Wood).

Out in the garden, or where you can feel really close to nature, place three red candles. These are your Fire totems. Place a glass bowl of blue water (coloured with woodstain dye or watercolours) in the space between the candles. Watch the light of the candle flames dance on the Water. Now sprinkle some of the Wood energy plants on to your Water magic, and finally a few more on to the lighted candles. You are symbolically offering up your own beauty to Water and Fire's natural balancers. As the aroma envelops you, affirm to yourself: 'I am of Wood, and of Wood will I explore the world. With freedom, with cooperation and with a greater desire for the love of humanity. This vision may be communicated with truth and honesty, vitalizing my inner world and my outer beauty.'

Summer season

Chakra is the Sanskrit word for 'wheel'. These wheels are energy centres located at seven invisible points extending from the base of your spine to the top of your head. These spirals of invisible energy vibrate and resonate to many other energies, corresponding and relating to all aspects of our lives. By working with each chakra in turn, you can awaken yourself to more positive energy. For beauty and harmony, you need to work on sensuality and charisma. When you are in a Wood phase or you feel a deep connection to Wood or it is your birth element, you need to work especially with the chakras that correspond to Fire and Water (see Diagram 6, page 82).

Here is a description of the chakra energy associations at their most simplified level:

Element Earth (Root chakra) – grounded, centred, waiting, acceptance

Element Water   (Sacral chakra) – receptive, creative, sensitive, sexual

Element Fire   (Solar Plexus chakra) – vitality, vision, enthusiasm, optimism

Element Wood   (Heart chakra) – detached love, compassion, ideals, altruism

Element Metal   (Throat chakra) – power, truth, trust, responsibility

The two other chakras are the Brow chakra (psychic, intuition, insight, spirit) and the Crown chakra (cosmic consciousness, soul, threshold). However, they are not associated with the Chinese elements. We have to work with the five elemental chakras. These correspond to our conscious knowledge, a self-awareness we must assimilate before we can move up to the higher chakras of the Brow and the Crown. These two bring us closer to an awareness of the unconscious, and beyond. The two chakras which are most important for Wood to vitalize are the Sacral chakra and the Solar Plexus chakra.

Sacral chakra

To bring harmony and balance to the Sacral chakra, gather fresh or dried lavender and sprinkle some of the flowers into a bowl placed on an east-facing

Five other chakras have been 'discovered' more recently, but for the purposes of our elemental journey we do not need to delve further into this highly regarded system of self-understanding, growth and healing.

window-ledge. Hang a bunch of lavender above your kitchen door for harmony, happiness and increased flexibility of mind.

If you can, acquire a piece of amber or aquamarine and place it in the most used room of the house. Each time you pass it, touch the crystal. Its power will energize your own inner senses. If you are Wood, you may think that intimacy with others means you will lose your freedom and be bound by responsibility and ties. However, by gently unblocking your Sacral chakra you can begin to understand that a relationship is not necessarily built on dependency. Others, also, may respect your individuality and need for freedom. To ensure that your seductive style and extrovert nature work for you, not against you, add rose geranium oil or a handful of rose petals to your bath-water before any close encounter that may be worrying you.

Solar Plexus chakra

The Solar Plexus chakra is where you can work with your ability to try out something new and to take risks, trusting in yourself to accept passion into your life. When you are Wood or in a Wood phase, although you may like to see change and progress in friends or partners, you rarely act impulsively or dynamically yourself! To ensure your Solar Plexus energy is unblocked so that progress can flow into your life, place a bloodstone, cornelian or piece of yellow citrine in the corner of your favourite room. All of these crystals represent clarity, vision and exuberance. Create a magic corner on a waist-high shelf. Place a small mirror behind your crystal to reflect its qualities back to you.

Earth season

For Wood the Earth season is the time to actualize your beauty and to reflect this in your home and surroundings. You don't have to redecorate the whole place, but by introducing some Feng Shui principles, you can start to balance the inner you with the outer world.

The best remedies and enhancements for Wood are chandeliers, candelabra and exciting lighting. Another good Fire balancer is a string of chillis hung in your kitchen to restore spirit and adventure to your relationships. If you don't have an open fireplace, hang paintings or photographs that contain some element of fire – anything from a mellow bonfire scene to a cosmic explosion of stars! Find an old piece of stained glass and lean it in a window to catch the sunlight and refract passion and excitement into your life.

You can also bring Water enhancements into your home, but avoid stagnant fish tanks! Alternatively, make your bath or shower an elegant place where you can enjoy the flow of Water. Otherwise, incorporate Water in the form of decoration – use rich blues, dark violets and blacks in fabric and furnishings. Add paintings and images of water – for example, old prints of dragonflies, frogs and toads, fish or deep-sea creatures and mermaids. Avoid too much Metal in your home as it is highly destructive to Wood and can lead you to believe there is no value in intimate relationships. A touch of Earth is always helpful to ground your big ideas and visions for the future. Choose one or two Earth colours, such as yellow ochre or terracotta. Place a group of pebbles near your main entrance to bring a sense of peace and purpose to everything you do.

Diagram 15
Wood's tree stone empowerment circle

Autumn

This is the best time of the year to work with self-empowerment for inner harmony. Metal rules the autumn season and is destructive to Wood in the elemental cycle. Wood people may often be engulfed by the potent self-assertion of Metal. Similarly, at this time of year, you may feel that your usual enthusiasm for freedom, for humanitarian and egalitarian goals is sapped by a sense of isolation. To enhance your own self-empowerment, harness the power of a Wood element empowerment circle (see Diagram 15).

Empowerment circles protect, inspire and nurture. By laying out an empowerment circle during the most difficult energy time of the year, you can reflect on your own qualities as well as combining them with those of the other elements. Thus, what was once an inauspicious period becomes a more beneficial time of year for planning and decision-making.

You can use any stones, pebbles, crystals or shells for your circle – in fact, any natural objects, as long as they are laid out in the way indicated. You may either leave the centre empty to meditate upon your dominant element or place your specific elemental talisman or crystal there as a reminder of your own value. The natural talisman for Wood is a pomegranate or apple. The crystal for Wood is malachite or green tourmaline.

If you create the circle outside your home, make sure it receives sunlight for at least some part of the day, as too much shade will have a depleting effect on its energy. If you create it inside your home, make sure it is in an east-facing room (east is Wood's empowering direction, especially in the autumn).

Keep the empowerment circle for most of the autumn or until you feel winter has finally arrived. Use the Fivefold Year calendar for Wood to remind you roughly when the change takes place. If you are aware of the changing phases of the moon, so much the better. At the full moon place a lighted green candle beside your empowerment circle and affirm to yourself: 'I am altruistic. My heart responds to the needs of mankind, and my vision is only for the goodness of the future.

My Wood is set alight with freedom, and my soul warms to the self-possessed.'

Once the nights begin to close in or you know that winter is just around the corner, you can safely clear away your empowerment stones or crystals. But keep them in a safe place (in a box or wrapped in silk). They are now your inner nourishers and must be respected as such.

Winter

Now is the time to work with your outer style and treat yourself with colours, enhancements and personal talismans. As an aesthetic and broad-minded extrovert, you need to express yourself in the most alluring and often experimental way. If you lean towards eccentricity, then use indulgent greens, deep turquoises, blacks, olives and exotic inky colours to enhance your cool perfection in style. Keeping your distance and maintaining your poise and glamorous appearance in any environment makes you irresistible. To enhance your seductive power in social encounters, wear simple, stark colours or erotic black to show you mean business. Carry or wear just one perfect crystal, such as a topaz, chalcedony or green tourmaline. To vitalize and nourish your inner beauty, take your natural talisman, a pomegranate (if you can't obtain pomegranates, use an apple), cut open the flesh and take out the seeds. When dry, place the seeds in a small stone or terracotta cup, close your eyes and count them one at a time. As you do so, imagine that each seed is offering you genuine compassion, attachment and sensitivity towards as many people you care about as there are seeds.

The Secret Chamber

Discovering your hidden qualities can enrich your whole sense of purpose in life. Each of us walks alone, aware of the world and everything in it only from our own viewpoint. The world centres around us, no matter how altruistic and charitable our manner. Even saints can see the world only from their saintly perspective, for they too are ego-centred.

This is why it is important to know how to channel your Wood energy in a positive way, not only to benefit yourself but also to enhance the energy system of the world as we know it. By seeing the virtues of your element as well as the defects, you can also begin to accept the disparity of others, as well as their connection with you.

Defects

If you're a Wood person, you may believe that your freedom must be maintained at all costs, even if this is at the expense of others' needs. Thus, you may reject any intimate contact, preferring detachment and cold response to warmth and the sharing of experience. You may feel you have the right to be different and expect others to honour this unique quality in you, yet deny it in themselves.

As a result, your relationships both with individuals and larger groups may suffer. If you stubbornly insist on impressing the world with your perfectionist ideals, you may be alienated by friends and family who have very different and equally valid ways of living their lives.

Virtues

By showing others how valuable informality and origi-
nality can be without offering your own as dogma,
and allowing others to express their own opinions, you
may find your own wisdom increases. Listen to the
knowledge of many minds. You have great powers of
individuality, more so than the other elements, and by
showing the value of independence to friends and colleagues you may inspire them with the sort of vision
for the future that is so deeply ingrained in your soul.
Your dynamic ability to objectify can bring about great
change within any group activity or partnership, and
so ensure that your own love of change manifests itself
in progress and reality rather than just the dreams and
aspirations in your head.

Chapter Eight

The Elements at Work

In this chapter discover the kinds of career, vocation or ways of working that best suit each birth element. If you are in a phase different from your birth element, then combine the two for a deeper insight into the best way of expressing your energy in the outer world.

Fire

As a Fire person, you may find you work best in a career where you are centre-stage, or certainly in charge – you need to lead, rather than be part of a team.

The entertainment industry is a wonderful place for you to release your exuberant and childlike energy. Teaching is also a good profession for those whose birth element is Fire, although you may lack the patience and tact to deal with young children. If you can balance your high-powered motivated energy with the benefits of Wood and Earth, you may find that your inspiration and vision can work well in all aspects of entrepreneurship or, literally, in front of the cameras!

To establish a more balanced and effective Fire energy in your career, try incorporating Earth and Wood into your environment by the inclusion of plants, and perhaps a small group of stones or carved sculpture, subtly placed in the office or working area. If you are working on stage or screen, in broadcasting or as a sales person, carry a piece of malachite or staurolite (fairy stone) in your pocket for added consistency and better tolerance of those around you who are less inspirational. It might be best to avoid working near water or with highly dominant Water people. They can literally drown your energy, and cause you to feel depressed and dissatisfied. This in turn can make you even more temperamental or prone to impulsive reactions, just to escape the waves of emotional energy surging around you.

Earth

Earth works best behind the scenes. You are able to take responsibility and to delegate it if the need arises. Having the power to control and discriminate means you can be gently assertive, confident that your ideas, schemes or plans are well thought out and based on practical common sense, rather than spontaneous and impulsive moments of irrational thinking. Your reliability means others will be comfortable with you, sure of your commitment and loyalty. Even though Fire colleagues may seem over-heated and too pushy, you will warm to their inspirational vision and be able to ground their ideas into practical benefits. Working with Wood people, however, may make you tear out your hair in frustration. You would prefer consistency and caution, autonomy and self-reliance than the liberal leanings of Wood. Wood can be too scattered and experimental in their pursuit of vocations that an Earth person knows take time to establish. If you can balance your sensible and yet highly developed artistic talent with the benefits of Fire and Metal enhancements in your environment, you may find that your self-reliance and persistence do pay off, when others would have impatiently given up on the job.

Bring Fire into your working environment by hanging a mirror behind your desk or work area. This deflects oppressive energy and encourages more dynamism into your workplace. Professions for Earth range from careers in such fields as management, economics or politics (for the more ambitious) to antique dealers, professional illustrators, artists, dancers and musicians. Outdoor Earth types may prefer gardening, landscape architecture or interior design.

Earth is more capable than any other element, but make sure that whichever career you are currently pursuing or are about to embark on fits your talent and your need for calm.

Metal

You may find you work best in a career where you can be in charge. You don't take lightly to being bossed around, and may find that teamwork or job-sharing responsibilities clash with your innate need to go it alone. Solitary and specialist work would suit you best. You are not naturally gregarious and would probably prefer to work behind the scenes manipulating big deals and guiding others to work on your behalf.

You need to maintain your detachment and self-possessed air in the big wide world, which means that you can be ruthless and ambitious when it suits you. You may find it awkward to be surrounded by too many Wood or Fire people. Fire people are inspiring and spontaneous, but their fiery and self-centred needs may conflict with your dedication to a cause, crusade or ambition. Metal expects achievement on a huge scale; Fire people strive simply for themselves.

The benefits of Water in the working environment can be huge for Metal. This reminds you of the need for communication and self-expression. You could find working in the healing professions particularily rewarding, as it exploits both your need to investigate, detect and observe and your ability to remain detached and calm in a crisis. You have a natural talent for listening, although you may find it hard to resist being a judge as well. However, Water people are invaluable in your chosen field, and you may well find you can balance the solitary compulsions of Metal with the necessary stamina and ability to regenerate, both physically and mentally. Detecting, investigation, research, marine occupations, dangerous missions, as well as financial advice and consultation, stock markets and gambling, are all professions to follow.

Blessed with the determination to work hard and long for your success, Metal people are never reliant on others for their future, or for encouragement and flattery, which is why they often have the reputation for working alone and for ruthlessness!

Water

Water must communicate. If it does not share in experience with others it will either turn to an iceberg of neuroses or an unstoppable tidal wave of frivolity. To enjoy your working environment you need people around you, providing you are free to go your own way if you feel a sudden unpredictable desire for change. A wide and varied workplace in the entertainment or media industries, where you can keep moving, is ideally suited to your restless nature. You may at times appear unreliable, ever ready to escape when others are heavily engaged by the challenges set them, but yours is the art of persuasion, imagination and creativity. Writing, journalism, speaking and the ability to express yourself are all valuable talents. You may prefer music to art, but any area where your creative ability is put to use will enhance and ensure you lead a peaceful and enjoyable employment.

Other careers that are suited to Water include the helping professions, therapies, psychology, counselling and nursing, as well as teaching, PR and dealing with the public. However, because of your acute awareness of others around you, it is important to take time out and relax in your own company.

Bring Wood into your working environment in the shape of wooden sculpture or an uplifting plant (avoid those that trail or cascade downwards, which can depress your changeable energy). Working with Fire people can wear you out, and Earth types may actually make you feel unable to move from your desk, or drain you of all your communicative skills. Wood people give you a sense of freedom from judgement, and Metal will inspire you to believe in yourself.

Wood

If you are a Wood person, you may find you work best in any environment where you can express as much freedom and individuality as you can. You have a flair for experimentation and innovation. With the ability to project long-term visions and ideas into the future, you may need a career which demands a scientific or re-search-based approach. More than anything, you require the scope to be inventive and original if you so choose. Your artistic side means you prefer an aes-thetically pleasing place to work. Perhaps your humanitarian values will pull you strongly towards working with social, world or environmental issues, where travel and the freedom to explore are prime requisites for your own love of non-commitment.

Working with Earth people can improve your need to ground your ideals and objectives, and Fire people may stimulate you to take risks and adopt a more ener-getic attitude to your plans. Water-type vocations involving one-to-one encounters – such as counselling and the helping professions – may seem attractive, but you would do better to have Water people around you rather than attempt to involve yourself personally. Therapies require a strong commitment to a close rela-tionship, something Wood people find uncomfortable even in their private lives.

Avoid working with Metal people; they conflict

with your idealistic visions by their seemingly invasive and arrogant sense of self-importance. If you are currently working in a difficult environment, improve your own self-esteem by carrying a piece of lapis lazuli or amber in your pocket or bag.

Anything from architecture to archaeology would suit you, but administration may prove a bore eventually. You need to enjoy the expansiveness of the world, to see others improving their life, health, social environment or vocation. Any career in which you can help people to improve their standard of living, either abroad or in this country, may provide a channel for your altruistic qualities.

The boss/employee relationship

How compatible with your employee/employer are you? Which of the other elements make the best work colleagues and how easily do you get along with those who may not see the world from your perspective? Use this section to help you deal with difficult relationships at work, establishing who may be your best boss or employer and highlighting those with whom you may come into conflict.

Fire boss/Fire employee

This could be an inspirational working arrangement, as long as both parties find the patience and discipline to accept one another's pushy and headstrong viewpoint. Taking a stand as a Fire employee could prove inhibiting and frustrating when confronted by an equally dominating Fire boss. Because they are so alike, the Fire employee might provoke and enjoy inciting their employer to the point of confrontation. Alternatively, the Fire boss could be so outrageously proud and self-centred that no Fire employee would be able to work under such a demanding and matched egotist. Fire needs to burn and burn alone. Together, they may blaze their way through the office, but they won't find it easy to relax in each other's company. Games of one-upmanship may ensue, in which the boss is always aware of their power and the employee always ready to test that they could be just as powerful! Fire is not happy as an employee and may resort to impulsive and risky tactics to assume the role of leader in the quest to get to the top, irrespective of anyone in the way. Although lacking Metal's ruthlessness, Fire people are just plain childlike in their need to be first and best!

Fire boss/Earth employee

This is a relationship that needs time to develop. Fire may assume that Earth is slow to catch on, perhaps lacking in vision or impact. However, the shrewd and sensible Earth employee usually checks out the territory first, establishing who holds the power and treading cautiously before asserting their own pressing need to be heard. Once Earth makes its own practical and grounded impact in the workplace, the Fire boss can relax and find Earth's company a comfortable and stimulating experience.

In response to Fire's wild and often impractical ideals, Earth can offer grounded advice and prudent observations that Fire might overlook in their headstrong approach to life. Pursuit is Fire's objective, while Earth prefers to wait and see. Together they can work on any project, in any environment, using each other's different energy levels to good effect. There may be times when Fire becomes frustrated by Earth's rigid and fixed opinions or commitment to the past. Fire would rather progress and move into a different gear, while Earth will prefer to stay with the security of what is known and true. Yet Earth will be encouraged and enchanted by the speed and and childlike antics of a Fire boss, and may develop a greater sense of achievement and the ability to take the initiative or risk without fear of the consequences.

Fire boss/Metal employee

The chances of Metal remaining Fire's employee for long are virtually nil. These are two extremists, and both require high degrees of respect from one another. Honour is a word that Metal uses a great deal, but if Metal doesn't respect Fire's rampant and sometimes explosive, daredevil energy, they may well leave their job and take the best team members with them!

Fire can inspire Metal to great things, but generally these two may find it difficult to adapt to one another's very different approaches to work. Ruthless in their own ambitions, Metal thrives on loyalty, power and determination. Fire is demanding, dynamic and a risk-taker; while Metal prefers to plan carefully, to scheme and to be certain before making any changes. Metal will want to run the show, and Fire may well allow Metal to take more responsibility than is necessary just to ensure Fire stays independent. Both equally determined and possessing a highly developed sense of self, the two egos may pull one another apart in a domination battle. Fire wants everything *now* and for itself, while Metal would rather dominate the world and teach it to sing the Metal way. Fire may not put up with the Metal dictatorial style for long, and firing may well be the result!

Fire boss/Water employee

Water is naturally communicative, expressive and sensitive. In any working environment where Fire is the boss, Water may find the high energy levels demanded of them quite exhausting.

Water is able to change, adapt and be flexible. This is an instant attraction for Fire, who will relish being with someone who is able to put up with their extraordinary impulsive outbursts and decisions at work. Fire and Water represent opposite energy levels: passionate and impulsive action versus unfocused and indecisive charm. Yet, somehow, in the workplace these two can temper one another, benefiting from each other's different energy.

Water can absorb Fire's often unrealistic demands, employing quick wits and clever planning to re-communicate the original idea in a form that Fire believes came directly from their own head. Water not only reassembles Fire's vision but adds an element of imaginative and sensitive thinking to enable the project, scheme or future investment to be realized. Water's communicative ability is something Fire values, often unconsciously. There is a danger, however, that Water can drown Fire in too much empathy for everyone else's problems.

Fire people need to be the centre of attention, to feed on the love of their employees, and expect total dedication from them. Water is too fickle, too inconsistent and unpredictable to vow loyalty to only one person, let alone an employer! Water can irritate Fire by being too introverted and apparently too charming. Water may well prove to be the agony aunt or uncle of the team, listening to everyone problem's including Fire's, which are usually the cause of many headaches. For their own part, Water people never give much away about themselves, and Fire doesn't mind this. But although Fire requires Water's flexibility, they may be too vain to handle Water's frivolity with the rest of the team.

Fire boss/Wood employee

This can be an excellent combination. In a working relationship the Fire boss may be a little too pushy for Wood who prefers procrastination to enthusiastic impulse. However, on the whole, Wood will be able to make compromises and accept the strident and fiery needs of their employer without being swayed from their own principles.

Wood functions best in work where the good of others is being served or nurtured. If Fire's vision and inspiration catches Wood's imagination, then together they can cooperate successfully and form a deeper connection than many other partnerships. The word partnership here is important, for Wood believes in equality. The only difficulty may be that Fire's enthusiasm for a new idea can fade as quickly as it blossomed. If Wood can't keep up with Fire's fast-paced schemes, then Fire may race off to the next idea before Wood has even had time to conceptualize the process. As a result, free-spirited Wood may be inclined to go their own way, detaching themselves and becoming overtly opinionated, just to ensure they maintain their freedom. Committing themselves to Fire's wild and often audacious visions could mean a loss of objectivity on Wood's part. Fire must learn to let Wood perfect and plan for the future in their own way.

But both will identify with the other and ensure a harmonious atmosphere, for both believe in freedom of the individual and are willing to experiment with new ideas. However, Wood won't be happy if Fire overloads the relationship with a power trip – the only thorn in Wood's altruistic, but ambivalent, side.

Earth boss/Earth employee

Earth has a passion for justification, perhaps the only dynamic that makes itself apparent in a usually cautious and receptive nature. But in an employer/employee relationship both may find they spend more time justifying themselves to each other than in any other mutual Earth relationship. The Earth employee lives up to the Earth boss's need for consistency, patience and pragmatism. Tolerance is the Earth employee's best attribute, apart from their artistic and creative nature, which needs something specific upon which to focus. If the Earth boss is in an acquisitive or indulgent mood, they may well offer their Earth employee a more valuable position or a move in the right direction. This confirms the Earth boss's need to feel secure. Feeling nourished by their chosen employees, Earth bosses are probably unique in rewarding their employees by ensuring they come even closer to their own desks. Remember, Earth people make careful employers, concerned primarily with their own security, particularly when it comes to trusting those around them, so an Earth employee is probably the only one they can trust.

However, Earth often suffers from a highly emotional and jealous nature. If neither boss nor employer is honest enough to admit to their fears and difficult feelings about their work or colleagues, then inner hostility and resentment may bubble to the surface. Earth people very rarely admit to being wrong, because they fear the consequences of having to live up to their word. In times of emotional turmoil Earth may prefer to walk out than admit to their Earth employer that their judgement was misguided.

Earth boss/Metal employee

One of the qualities that the Earth boss admires most is persistence, and Metal is intensely persistent. Indeed, this can be so extreme at times that even Earth may begin to wonder what it is that drives Metal on.

Earth may find a Metal employee difficult to work with. Earth thrives on hard work, and is resilient to the most egotistic of self-starters and ruthless individuals. But Metal's single-minded, egocentric world can push Earth's usually reserved and contained nature into a whirl of unstable self-protection. Metal can make Earth believe that there may be someone after his job. Metal is naturally ambitious, determined to get to the top, even if it means shaking Earth's usually solid ground in the process. Earth people may be able to handle this minor blip in their usually passive world but only if they realize that Metal needs a strong container from which to emerge. Earth people, if they play their hand right, could provide this ideal environment, and as long as Earth makes sure Metal climbs to the top of someone else's ladder, they'll be friends for life.

Earth may deny their own self-centred need for power. Craving security more than anything else, occupying a position at the top often demands more than Earth's emotional nature can handle. Power necessarily brings with it the chance that you may fall, and with Metal around, Earth may feel decidedly like Humpty Dumpty on the wall! Yet Earth can also benefit from Metal's own resilience and dedication to any job or cause in which they are involved, and will be an undoubted asset to any team or creative enterprise that Earth has in mind.

Earth boss/Water employee

Earth's natural inclination is to live in the here and now, to trust in the evidence, rather than in ephemeral ideas and the world of intuitive guesswork. When an Earth employer works with Water they may find a distinctly different approach, not only in their way of thinking but in their very way of being. Water is flexible; Earth is fixed. Earth demands consistency; Water actively seeks out change.

In some ways Earth can benefit and learn from Water's immeasurable imagination and gifts of communication and sensitivity. In turn, Water may also respond to Earth by recognizing the necessity to focus and concentrate on a given task, rather than rushing off in a different direction. But Earth soaks up Water, and in the workplace the Earth boss may easily dry up Water's light-hearted attitude to life, so much so that Water soon feels it has to escape from commitment to any responsibility. Water would rather communicate, functioning as a conduit or a catalyst for ideas and schemes, than take responsibility for their successful operation. Commitment and dedication are not particularly favourite words in the Water employee's vocabulary; however, persuasion, ingenuity and transience are.

Earth may find Water exhausting as they constantly run round after Water, clearing up unfinished work and being faced with unpredictable dilemmas. Water, too, may tire of Earth's cautious and narrow-minded approach to the job, yet by drawing on Earth's wisdom and enterprise, Water can learn much about trust and develop a greater sense of focus.

Earth boss/Wood employee

Wood has a natural instinct for making Earth people feel good about themselves. Earth is highly receptive, and values work colleagues who are trustworthy, efficient, cool and unemotional. Earth people have enough problems with their own feelings, and in the workplace they prefer the easy-going atmosphere that Wood employees can bring. However, the drawback for Wood is that Earth is deeply principled and unwilling to change. In contrast, Wood employees like to see change around them, favouring growth, a change of ethics, fairly apportioned job-sharing schemes and team equality and meetings that include everyone in the company. This sense of universal equality and fairness is one with which Earth may have trouble coming to terms. Earth values fairness, but on a one-to-one basis only.

Wood people have much to offer Earth, for they are artists of diplomacy, geniuses who require little organization. Earth prefers to avoid conflicts, and Wood people are easily persuaded to respond to Earth's good-natured and pragmatic ways, as long as what they are doing has some long-term value or worldwide application. The problem arises when Wood derives no satisfaction from working for Earth. Earth may then represent conventionality and barriers that must be broken down. Wood people fiercely respect their own freedom and differences, and if the Earth boss is not amenable to this kind of individualist streak, they may come to blows with the more eccentric and opinionated tests that Wood likes to set for their adversaries!

Earth boss/Fire employee

Whenever Earth feels certain that the time is ripe for careful planning or shrewd investment, the chances are Fire will leap forward with another daring and optimistic idea ahead of everyone else. Earth may prefer to move carefully when making deals, creating new boundaries or expanding the company. But Fire, if true to form, will, with impatient and highly motivated urgency, urge Earth to just get on and do it! In such a relationship Earth may begin to grow resentful of Fire's never-ending enthusiasm for new ventures. Fire may well have talents in the role of a generator of ideas and visions, but they are hopeless at completing and consolidating once the initial activity has ceased. Earth knows this, and may use Fire's exuberant spirit in areas of work that call for forward thinking. However, Earth will shrewdly place the responsibility of seeing the process through in the hands of another Earth or a Metal employee.

Fire is an excellent negotiator for Earth's sometimes uneasy and distant approach to others. Fire people gamble, speak their mind, are tactless and yet passionate about the truth. This gives Earth the chance to negotiate from behind the scenes. Rivalry may develop, however, if Fire ever achieves the same status or joins the boardroom meetings with Earth. Earth people are intensely jealous of such a high-spirited nature, and will hold on tenaciously to their job if Fire ever threatens to rise in flames near Earth's sacred altar of power.

Metal boss/Metal employee

Metal people respect other Metal types, simply because they know how powerful is their own dedication to ambition and success. This highly charged and sometimes emotive relationship works best if both are honest enough to declare their ambitions and agendas on first meeting. If anyone can put up with a Metal employee, a Metal boss can! For here, the clash of Metal can prove a most effective weapon for both. The Metal boss may certainly be kept on their toes, and the Metal employee would enjoy the challenge posed by someone higher up the ladder than themselves.

Both are loners, and could make a powerful, autonomous team if they understand that the other's compulsive arrogance factor is as high as their own. This could be difficult for the Metal boss, in particular, as they probably achieved their current position through ruthless agility, extremist tactics and astute planning. A Metal employee is just as capable of the same strategy! Metal regenerates, and both are capable of pushing the other to the limit until one is destroyed or has no option but to retaliate. Both have recuperative and realistic powers at hand. Neither will be thwarted, and neither will lose. If they can understand that they share the same fear of exposing their emotional vulnerability and that over-achievement is a compensation for inner loneliness, perhaps they can forge their careers together to reflect their search for high esteem and power.

Metal boss/Water employee

This could be a genuinely successful, long-term combination if both feel their work together has some deeper connection. Metal thrives on Water's ability to adapt, to flow in and out of places that Metal would find uncomfortable. Metal is acutely aware of the importance of recognizing the changes and nuances in business enterprises, the financial stakes and the need to take chances, but not so able to sense human fallibility. Water has the ability to sense every mood change, to intuit the thoughts, feelings and ideas of others and of the *Zeitgeist*. Metal would find Water a valuable ally in any dealings where risk or compromise were needed. Water easily goes with the flow, whereas Metal finds it easier to maintain its own flow. Thus, a Metal boss can easily rely on Water's judgement in playing the market or any innovative creative endeavour. Water also communicates with ease and alacrity, something for which Metal has little time, nor much natural talent. Metal's instinct for survival rubs off on Water, and can allow Water to follow their particular dream without fear of being punished for unpredictability. Metal knows that to survive you must follow your instincts, and Water's elusive and sometimes fickle behaviour serves to remind Metal that what goes around, comes around!

The only problem this relationship can pose is if Water decides to be too gregarious and compliant, trying to be everything to everyone. Then, Water could become slippery, underhand and deceitful, unsure of where their real loyalty lies. At this point Metal must choose between integrity and frivolity. It is fairly obvious which button Metal will press!

Metal boss/Wood employee

A sticky relationship that requires tact and diplomacy on the part of Wood if it is to succeed. However, Wood is ably suited to stroking Metal's ego in all the right places. Although Wood people are just as egocentric as Metal, they have a knack for responding to the demands of Metal without causing too much friction, as long as they know it's for the good of the whole company, project, vision or simply mankind. Wood has a remarkable sympathy with the world, but Metal is the most likely of all the elements to arouse frustration and stress in Wood with their assertive and greedy agenda. Wood will consider the Metal boss to be ruthless, underhand and inflexible but may admire Metal's rise to superiority and acknowledge their dedication, success and power. If Metal can only honour Wood's own values of personal freedom, detachment and social adeptness, the Metal boss may find Wood a valuable member of the team. But Wood needs an open house in which to operate, not Metal's conveyor-belt factory.

Wood may see the Metal boss as someone bereft of a social conscience. But what Metal does have is an equally high standard of moral and ethical conduct, even though this may be more autonomous and self-possessed than Wood's group-conscious approach to life. Conflicts will surely arise at some point when Wood decides to override brainwaves with practical strategy. A Metal boss needs to be surrounded by dynamic and enthusiastic energy, and Wood's experimental methods may not live up to Metal's faith in spontaneous inspiration.

Metal boss/Fire employee

Metal excels at being in power, and Fire insists on leading or being the centre of attention. This is fine if the Metal boss is happy for Fire's audacity and brilliance to shine out as a selling tool for their own business or profession. Fire can work wonders for Metal's sense of distinction. The Metal boss may lack poise and grace in handling situations and would rather get straight to the point. Fire, if allowed to blaze with pure inspiration and enthusiasm for the job, can instil a sense of vision that Metal often lacks. Both these elements are arrogant and self-aware: Fire people want the best and believe themselves to be the best; Metal knows what is best and how to achieve it. This subtle difference shows when Metal sets out on one of their crusades for a cause, putting all their integrity behind it. Fire just goes out for what they want for self, and self alone.

As an employee, Fire can greatly benefit from observing Metal's ability to hold back, knowing precisely the right moment for making choices. Fire often loses out through impulsive action, and then may simply shrug and look for another chance. Although Metal will never let an opportunity pass and may find Fire's willingness to take yet another risk infuriating, Metal can be enlightened by Fire's motivation. Metal may also be very wary of Fire's competitive spirit, often employing underhand tactics to ensure that Fire doesn't oust them from their own powerful position. Together, they could stimulate and create enough challenges to work well as a team, but both must beware of blunt speaking and proud vanity.

Metal boss/Earth employee

The Metal boss can gain much satisfaction from employing Earth in his professional interests, business or influences. The benefits for Earth are equally auspicious, as Earth must feel secure and needed in any workplace. Metal offers loyalty mixed with dedication and shrewd thinking. For Earth, feeling valuable and committed to any cause Metal has in mind will stimulate Earth's appetite for creative and practical craftsmanship.

Earth can be a useful support when Metal feels insecure or challenged, instilling a sense of consistency and diligence in Metal's sometimes very lonely life. With Earth, Metal also feels less vulnerable to competition or an insidious will. Knowing that Earth respects and enjoys the luxury of a close working relationship, Metal may offer Earth more than might be expected from such a remote and apparently self-centred individualistic boss, and Earth's love of the here and now will help alleviate any anxieties Metal may have for the future. On the whole, this is a two-way ride to a harmonious and usually highly profitable working relationship. Both like to make money and are unlikely to fritter it away on unnecessary speculation.

Water boss/Water employee

Although both have a natural empathy for the other, this scatty combination is likely to produce little work, preferring instead to play and seizing any opportunity to avoid getting down to the mundane practicalities of life.

Water people are more likely to be involved in an industry that views fun and entertainment as work: the media, arts, publishing, travel, PR – all professions where business can be conducted at a flexible and social level. The chances of finding these two together is high, as this is the most gentle working relationship of all the elements.

The Water boss may well feel more relaxed and at ease with the imaginative and suitably entertaining Water employee. There is little threat here of being taken over or undermined. Water is not ambitious, preferring instead to enjoy life, to socialize and live a fairly gregarious and romantic existence. Water is not out for excessive gain and would probably prefer the social side of business lunches, gossip and behind-the-scenes romances to the up-front dedication of high-powered executives. Water, as a boss, may find Water employees the easiest to control, as management is not something Water takes to. Supervision means responsibility, delegation and commitment – all things that make it virtually impossible to escape for a long weekend! Water and Water together make pleasing companions, too. They are capricious and changeable, and the Water boss can sympathize with his employee's need for unpredictability and inconsistent behaviour. Water, more than any other element, has an acutely psychic awareness of others around them, and for this reason may find another Water in their camp a mirror for their own anxieties.

Water boss/Wood employee

The Water boss can appear fickle, restless and changeable to those employees who see only the more neurotic tendencies of Water surface when under pressure. Water's true talent is for communication, intellectual consideration and for seduction, all characteristics that make Water often unconsciously rise to the top in their profession. Water doesn't go out looking for power, but when they tumble into such a position, they revel in the flexibility and entertainment it provides them. A Wood employee may view Water as highly adaptable, over-sensitive and opportunistic. but Wood can benefit from Water's more amiable side and preference for one-to-one relationships. Although Wood sees the big picture, they sometimes find it hard to look at individuals as individuals, preferring to believe that what is good for the masses is good for the individual. A Water boss can temper Wood's rather reformist and compartmentalized attitude to life.

On the other hand, Wood, as an employee, has much to offer Water. They can guide Water to use their incredibly clever minds and persuasive tactics for wider ranging and futuristic expansion. Wood may prefer to take a back seat and guide, in their group-conscious way, from within the team or from the wings. But Wood's art of diplomacy in business and pleasure provides scope for Water to escape the harsh realities of day-to-day pressure. For Water lives in the world of dreams, not conflict and manoeuvres. Water may have perfected the art of getting themselves out of difficult situations, but they need to find a space away from the madding crowd for a while. Wood's unbiased and broad-minded vision will enable Water to leave the desk unattended, knowing Wood will be there when they return from dreamland.

Water boss/Metal employee

Metal's hunger for power may interfere with a passive and impressionable Water boss, if the latter hasn't already tuned into Metal's psyche. But Water usually manages to pick up the vibrations of whoever they meet faster than they can actually untangle their own thoughts. If Water knows that Metal's extreme nature is for the good of the industry or profession in which they are engaged, then Water has the persuasive charm and adaptability to lure Metal into a far more artful trap. For Water is a trickster, whereas Metal is straight down the line. Metal is a conformist, attracted by glamour, by money, by power; Water simply plays with life's experiences, and can charm their way in and out of any professional crisis.

Once Water has become familiar with the machinations of Metal, they can begin to respond to each other with fairness and frankness, making use of each other's very different qualities. Metal demands all or nothing in the fight for success and can show Water how to make decisions and take opportunities without feeling guilty for not being nice in the process. Water, on the other hand, can add a touch of humour and wit to every occasion, giving Metal a chance to realize that life and work do not necessarily have to be so serious. The only problem will arise when Metal wants Water's job, but by then Water will probably have cunningly moved on anyway, just in the nick of time!

Water boss/Earth employee

When Water is confronted by an accumulative mass of earth it tends either to seep its way slowly through the soil or gather like a tidal wave and sweep across the top. However, the Water boss is likely to do neither when confronted by the grounded and habit-bound Earth employee. Water may find it preferable to leave the office rather than face the side of Earth that simply 'knows best'. Water wants to try out new ideas, shape the imagination and keep moving, rather than sink into the mud of an Earth employee's preoccupation with management, materialism and getting it right.

A Water boss is rarely interested in the rights and wrongs of every application, and would prefer to be inspired by the risk of Fire than the pragmatic and structured indulgences of Earth. Earth may equally find a Water boss's inconsistency and inability to commit themselves to any course of action exasperating. Working for the most unpredictable and changeable boss they've ever met will infuriate Earth, who wants stability and precision. Unless there are a few Fire employees around to relieve the tension or a strong Metal personality to keep Water on their toes, Earth may complain too much about the loose ends, and Water may escape and let everyone else get on with it, thus opening themselves up to manipulation by others.

Water boss/Fire Employee

Water must communicate, whether by mouth or on paper, but the often tactless and blunt remarks of a Fire employee are enough to give the Water boss sleepless nights worrying about how to get round this brash self-starter.

Fire wants to be best and wants to lead. Fire people are acutely ambitious, preferring to pioneer and explore rather than negotiate and impress. All this rampant and often flamboyant energy can whirl Water into a hysterical and neurotic state. While Water likes to be inspired, something Fire can do better than any other element, Water doesn't appreciate Fire's displays of immature dramatics in the boardroom, office or social settings. In turn, Fire may grow weary of Water's indecisive and unfocused ideology, and impatiently negotiate deals, investments or mergers without even asking for Water's advice or approval. This could lead to a competitive and highly charged atmosphere, one that Fire will thrive on but in which Water may feel distinctly pushed out in the cold. Prone to periods of low self-esteem and faced by an employee who is interested only in making the future rosy for themselves, Water could get even more non-commital just for the sheer hell of it. But together they have much to offer if they can learn to respect each other's differences. Fire's complacent and yet stylish manner can work wonders in all social situations and group encounters. Water is excellent in one-to-one communication and may teach Fire to burn brightly, but it will have to be with respect and sensitivity to their superiors.

Wood boss/Wood employee

Two similar elemental types have an innate empathy for one another. The Wood boss may respond to the Wood employee as just another extension of their own enterprising success story. Wood is able to reap the rewards of their work, being controlled, detached and confident that human emotions and games won't interfere in their quest for truth and freedom. Both may enjoy the courtesy and informality of working with one another. For out of all the elements, this working relationship will seem more like an equal partnership. The Wood boss is always ready to consider new ideas, experiments and unconventional methods. To be surrounded by Wood employees will enable the Wood boss to offer as much freedom to those who are genuinely altruistic as he would to himself. Wood is group-conscious, and together they can progress with highly sophisticated skills to master the art of social interaction as a means to success. They may at times prefer to detach themselves from one another in their working relationship, but each will always respect the other's need for perfection. Their only problem is pro-crastination, and often the job never gets off the ground even though they are extrovert go-getters. Wood is so stubbornly opinionated that they may argue over the most basic of issues.

Wood boss/Fire employee

The Wood boss, for all their apparent ambivalence, is notoriously egotistic. They have high standards and strong moral and ethical values, which are not appar-ent on the surface and can in extreme circumstances make them powerful fighters for a cause. A Fire em-ployee is probably one of the few who can provide Wood with the necessary enthusiasm and excitement to really enjoy the self-control required to keep them at the top.

Being strongly in favour of change and transfor-mation, Wood will enjoy the daredevil and sometimes pushy attempts of a Fire employee to get things mov-ing. Fire's dynamic and urgent sense of progression can allow Wood the luxury of really seeing the wood for the trees! Fire may also benefit from Wood's self-possessed wisdom and insight. Faced by Fire's often unbearably childlike demands for more, Wood can detach themselves for the good of the whole, and per-haps offer Fire a chance to see themselves from a different and less selfish viewpoint. Fire gives to the cause, as long as there is a new cause to follow, and Wood can always find a new opening for Fire, simply because Fire burns and assumes there will be one!

Wood boss/Earth employee

Although these are two very different types, both in their motivation and thinking, the Earth employee may well find, to begin with at least, the more controlled nature of the Wood boss a safe option. The problems may arise when Earth begins to draw attention to the facts and figures, concerned to build concrete and contained agendas out of the Wood boss's scattered and liberal schemes.

Wood excels at working for the good of the group: humanitarian and social issues are food for its ambitions. However, Earth is self-righteous when it comes to change and won't easily accept the eccentric methods of Wood's forward planning. Earth can become habit-bound in their day-to-day work, much to the annoyance of Wood, who would rather communicate with those who thrive on informality and need a broad-minded base from which to work. Earth people are narrow-minded when it comes to straying beyond their own territory, and may recoil from what they see as any dissident form of behaviour. It may be that they can learn much from one another's differences, but both are, in their different ways, as self-willed as the other, and Earth may eventually resign rather than follow lofty schemes that mean nothing to them.

Wood boss/Water employee

The gypsy quality of Water's entertaining and beguiling spirit may lure Wood into responding with equal openness in the workplace. Usually, Wood enjoys the company of those able to express themselves in tidy packages. However, although Water may expand and stretch, bend and distort many of their meetings and conversations out of all proportion, Wood somehow delights in this witty and highly vivacious employee. Because they get on so well, this may become more of a friendship than a distinct boss/employee relationship. Wood loves to see others change and to witness progress and development in the world. Water is highly changeable, thus providing Wood with the necessary outlet through which to channel their ideas and maverick schemes.

Clearly equipped with the charm to sell most people their ideas, Water can also convince themselves their own dreams will come true. They are romantics after all. Here, Wood can offer Water a lesson in self-deceit. Although Wood may vacillate when it comes to spontaneous action, they always know the answers to the biggest questions and can predict future consequences. For the Water employee this is a chance to learn that drifting from dream to dream isn't always the best way to realize your deepest desires.

Wood boss/Metal employee

This relationship needs careful attention. This applies not so much to Metal, who is dedicated to any cause that Wood puts forward in the boardroom or office, but to Wood, who may be in danger of losing an inner battle with the Metal employee. Wood may neither know nor care about Metal's darker ambitions and manipulative actions. Wood tends to try to see the good in everyone first before judging them, hoping that the person will either redeem or condemn themselves before Wood has to make a decision. But Metal is shrewd, undermining and power-conscious when driven. Metal wants to be in control, and has the arrogance and the integrity to achieve this, even in a subtle and underhand way. This is when Wood must watch their backs. Metal's ambitions do not stop at the boss's door. When Metal isn't glamorizing the power of their future success, they make excellent lone players, able to work through any crisis and dedicated to the system. But Metal people are inflexible and highly critical of themselves as well as others. Wood, too, is intolerant of anything short of perfection when in sour mood, and they may clash in their views and general outlook on life more often than is beneficial for Wood's liberal nature.

Chapter Nine

The Elements as Lovers and Partners

Use this guide to determine how well your element resonates with that of your lover or partner. Compatibility here is, of course, generalized. The five elements of Feng Shui are part of a larger system of Chinese astrology, and there are many other factors to be considered in your birth chart. This is an introductory guide, based only on your birth element. However, if you currently feel strongly in tune with another element, then refer to that mode of expression.

Fire man/Fire woman

When these two first meet, they may stimulate each other into taking all kinds of risks and adventures. Romance will be the motivation for every activity they share, and they are likely to fall in love quickly. As with any double dose of elemental energy, they have a natural affinity and empathy for one another. However, the test is likely to arise if one becomes bored and starts looking elsewhere. The Fire man is always on a quest for ideal love, but the Fire woman is more likely to abandon the search if her Fire man runs out of fuel she needs to keep her fantasies stoked up.

They are both childlike in the extreme, so wild provocations, games and romantic gestures will typify their relationship initially. The Fire woman is just as pushy as the Fire man, and whoever makes the first move is likely to hold the reins of power. This partnership could easily turn into a power struggle to find out who is the most dynamic, impulsive and dramatic. But because either can respond with an intuitive knack for saying the right thing just at the right time, they may be able to overcome any difficult moments when the other becomes too outrageous or audacious.

Two such passionate people together can ignite a lot of anger around them. They may find their friends, family and possible competitors enraged by their apparent brash and tactless approach. Fire is jealous when riled, and if anyone can provoke a Fire woman into a dominating role, a Fire man surely can. But the Fire woman will make sure that her Fire man is hers and hers alone.

Fire people always know where they want to go next in any relationship. The problem is they may both want to go in different directions, for independence is essential for them both. As much as they need a long-term partner, Fire can begin to feel restricted and claustrophobic if the relationship isn't constantly on the move. This is why, sexually, they need so much fantasy, imagination and inspiration in their love-making. Neither is keen on emotional scenes, commitments or exposing their feelings. Theirs must be a relationship of dreams and wild abandon, of impulsive sexual encounter and images to love by. Their urgency has led them to many changes in sexual direction, but if they can keep up with one another theirs will be a fun-loving and passionate partnership.

Fire woman/Earth man

This is a difficult relationship for the Fire woman, mostly because her Earth man may find it hard to live up to her energetic lifestyle.

When they first meet, Earth will want to take his time, while the Fire woman will blaze into his life like a raging inferno. Curiously attracted to something so irresistibly exciting, he may find himself involved before his usually cautious head has had time to think. Reeling backwards from the first force of the Fire woman's passion is enough to trap him, but the Earth man may find it hard to indulge in this kind of exhausting mental and physical game for long. The Fire woman will want to express herself, and is often blunt and tactless in public. The Earth man would rather keep himself to himself.

The Earth man will also insist that he is right and knows what's best for them both, which the Fire woman may find hard to live with. Her independence and need to dominate could course a few angry scenes concerning his tenacity and her immaturity. The Earth man likes to think he is grown up, whereas the Fire woman doesn't want to grow up at all. The other conflict they might encounter is over money. The Earth man may want to handle the cash flow, but she would rather just spend it!

Sexually, they may be extremely compatible. The Earth man is a sensualist in the extreme, and although he may tire of her urgent desires and childlike sexual games, he'll be fascinated by her extraordinary imagination and stimulating company. The Earth man can provide a cosy and safe nest for the Fire woman if she truly wants it. With the quiet back-up of this sensual man, she can take off into the realms of fantasy without alarming anyone.

The Earth man possesses a grounded serenity, providing a peaceful container for Fire's vulnerable 'little-girl-lost side' that hides beneath the cloak of her furiously independent spirit. Sexually they are so complementary that they might find it difficult to live without each other's balancing energy levels. If the Fire woman can begin to realize that the Earth man's caution could provide her with security, and if he, in turn, recognizes that her impetuous will could give him the pleasures of a truly hedonistic life, they will have a superb future together.

Fire man/Earth woman

For the impatient, dramatic and pushy Fire man, a warm, sensual, earthy woman is an unimaginable find. And the Fire man loves the unimaginable! The Earth woman is looking for a rock-solid relationship, one where she can share her feelings, her troubles and her heart as well as her bed. She may well fall passionately in love with the Fire man just because he is so different – funny and optimistic, he is life's clown and everybody's friend. But the Earth woman will want exclusivity, which for the Fire man would prove too constricting. Requiring plenty of room to breathe, he must be able to take risks if he chooses and be inspired by all of life.

When they first meet, they may be besotted by each other's apparent differences. Opposites do attract! The Earth woman may enjoy his glamorous, go-getting attitude, and fall for his passionate and dynamic lovemaking. But she could also tire of his vanity and self-centredness. The Earth woman needs friendship, loyalty and total commitment. She likes to immerse herself in the process of loving, in the emotions and undercurrents of the relationship, not just the physical act itself. This may work while Fire is high on the buzz of the romance, but to go beyond the heady irrational moments of first love could prove draining for Fire and painful for Earth.

Emotionally, Fire can't submit to a possessive woman, and will certainly resist commitment. Yet he will burn for her sensual and sexual prowess, yearn for her in his fantasies and dreams. Whether he can find room in his life for her as well as everything else is questionable.

The price she will have to pay for his love is to grant him the freedom to roam. The Fire man is not particularly interested in a close family life, and hasn't the sensitivity to understand Earth woman's deeper needs. But, given a loose rein, he may return to her with warmth and loyalty again and again.

Fire woman/Metal man

The Fire woman loves to attract, and she certainly won't have much trouble exciting the heart and soul of the deadly powerful Metal man. Indeed, he may find her impromptu and carefree spirit a positive challenge, for a Fire woman can provoke in him a powerfully erotic desire. The Metal man is highly sexed, and may well be more interested in the physical relationship than anything else. This relationship is often an extremely sexual and torrid one. Emotionally, they may drain each other dry with their intense passion for life. For the Metal man, what counts are big truths, deep confessions and the darker aspects of life. The Fire woman wants to enjoy and revel in life's pleasures not to be drawn into the depths of pain and suffering, emotional scenes and melancholia. The Fire woman loves dangerous living, never giving a moment's thought to the implications of her actions. The risk is what counts to her – the superficial dangers, not the depths. For the Metal man, however, what counts is the danger beneath the surface, the pain and the secrets of the night, and the Fire woman may have to work hard to handle his soul-searching ultimatums. Nevertheless, he may well prove to be the best physical relationship she's ever had.

If there is a strong magnetic attraction between these two, it may become permanent if both learn to give each other enough space to clarify their own needs. Metal is terribly autonomous, while Fire is highly demanding and needs to be the centre of attention. He is all or nothing, erotic and power-hungry. She is dynamic, arrogant and often pushy. Both are determined, each with a highly developed sense of self. For Metal and Fire to fuse in a joint and long-term partnership, they must learn to realize their mutual need for domination.

Handled with care this could be an exciting and dramatic relationship, but this kind of intensity must be acknowledged and expressed. The Fire woman is always out for herself and will not be bossed around or play submissive. Confronted by her passion for life and her extravagance, Metal man may not feel sufficiently in control. Without a sense of power, he may destroy their intimacy just as quickly as it blazed into his life. However, if he can assert his own demands truthfully and still honour hers, theirs may be a powerful compelling relationship.

Fire man/Metal woman

The intangible and mysterious quality of the Metal woman is without doubt one of the first things a Fire man will be attracted to. He may find romancing with such a secretive and yet erotic woman the biggest thrill he has ever had. Equally, she may find his fiery passion irresistible, and he'll respond to those dark erotic messages with true Fire-like arousal. Like the Metal man and Fire woman combination, this is a relationship brimming with sexual passion and the power struggles that go with it. Initially, the Fire male may well assume this is the love of his life, only to have his doubts as the relationship develops.

The Fire man believes he is the only male capable of attracting this kind of woman. However, when he does, he may well get caught up in her plans for deeper involvement, which will prove incompatible to his independent ego. The Metal woman is always fixed in her desires, and her relentless, all-or-nothing love for the Fire man may prove a restricting test. Capable of making great sacrifices to keep him in her territory, she can also be secretly destructive to herself and the relationship if she's not getting what she wants. Her melancholic periods may drive him mad, because fun and enjoyment are what this man lives for. Equally, she may grow weary of his tactless, brash assumptions and outrageous judgements and of the way he spends more time prancing in front of the mirror and phoning his friends than listening to her ambitions for the future!

On the other hand, Metal women admire self-starters. She will love his dynamism, his ability to say exactly what he means and his stylish and flamboyant love-making. Sexually, they can do wonders for each other, even though their inner needs are very different. On the surface they seem to share the same ambitions and need for personal success, but the Metal woman is not averse to manipulating the affair and diversifying for her own ends. The Fire man can be the loyalest of lovers, but is just as likely to fall in love with someone else in yet another moment of rash, over-heated passion.

Fire woman/Water man

The Fire woman is usually pretty sure where she is going next, for she regards life as an adventure. When she bumps headlong into a Water man, their very contradictory natures might seem totally overwhelming. The flow of energy between them may, at first, be uneasy, but the tension could well produce remarkable results if they play the right games. The Fire woman will want to run the show and lure the highly impressionable and responsive Water man into her arms as quickly as she can. The Water man will, of course, be interested in her body, but may prefer to dally awhile, fascinated by what is going on inside her beautiful, fiery head. He may find her bossy, straightforward approach to life refreshing. Thriving on change and the flow from mellow to dynamic energy, he will find that the Fire woman can certainly provide him with enough challenges to keep him entertained, and he will want to improve upon every one she makes.

Their main problem is that the Fire woman may want to upgrade her Water man. By nature she needs to lead, to activate and to initiate, actions that the Water man would prefer to avoid. While he certainly needs plenty of intellectual stimulation, communication and romance, he does not relish being driven at a pace he cannot enjoy. Water goes with the flow, but if the flow gets too fast and furious, he'll simply escape to calmer waters for a while.

She may have to accept that at times he will prefer to listen to her friends talk about their latest love lives than gaze into her beautiful eyes all night. She is jealous, he is not. She wants the limelight, to be the centre of attention, while he may prefer to flirt and laugh with every girl around. It's not that he is promiscuous, just that he loves to soak up the atmosphere. Water's nature means that there will be times when Fire's powerful spirit and demanding nature forces him to retreat. Theirs could be a sexually exotic relationship, as long as the Fire woman accepts that Water subjects involve their mind, soul and heart as well as their body, and that love is about the mutual awareness of each other's needs.

Fire man/Water woman

For all their astounding incongruities – indeed, maybe because of them – these two are usually unable to resist one another. The Water woman is a gregarious, social animal, and the chances are she'll often bump into the Fire man during her transient and ever-changing life. She may even be the one to make the first move, as she's noted for her persuasive charm, especially when bedazzled by the passionate urgency of a Fire man. He, of course, will be fascinated by her changeable and unpredictable nature, and together they may find romantic adventure in everything they do. However, frustration and irritation may build up for him when her inconsistent desires and often capricious moods and feelings seem to centre on everyone else except him. The Fire man's ego needs polishing more than any other element – if not all of the time, then often – and Water women can't be bothered to polish anything!

The Water woman is a good listener, and may spend the evening helping her friends to understand their problems or gossiping with her sister's boyfriend on the phone. Unfortunately, Fire is jealous of the Water woman's capacity to give herself and her time freely to others, whether male or female. She is a flirt when she chooses, and if the Fire man is too possessive or tactless, she may escape to the arms of a less dominating and self-absorbed lover.

When they work together they work well. Sexually, they are a potent concoction, and Fire's enthusiastic love-making can inspire and free the Water woman from any sexual hang-ups. Neither element is interested in great displays of emotion. Water has deep feelings that she prefers not to reveal to herself, let alone her lover, while Fire just hasn't got the time even to acknowledge he has them. The sadness is that both are vulnerable and refuse to admit it to each other. Happily, however, their childlike sense of fun may keep them going through the long nights. Secret meetings, sexual experiences while travelling and impulsive moments will be shared with the delight of two souls who draw out the best from one another, if only they dare. Fire might do so, but will Water?

Fire woman/Wood man

It has been known for the Wood man, for all his aloof glamour and high ideals, to be led astray by the headstrong and wilful Fire woman, perhaps the only woman who can do this. This is a combination that works well, and if the Fire woman is patient (not easy for her, but worth the wait), she'll be rewarded with a wonderful lover and a free-spirited, sophisticated and non-dominating partner. The Wood man may put off any involvement with the Fire woman for as long as he possibly can. It's not that he isn't attracted by her grace, passion and audacity, but that he really wants to make sure first that they can be friends.

A short, sharp sexual relationship is not often high up the list in a Wood man's mental notebook. He is a perfectionist after all, which means taking time, analysing and checking out all the possible motives before he'll leap in the flames. For the Fire woman, this man seems ideal. He's freedom-loving, detached and glamorous. Yes, she needs romance, but she also adores his brain, gets off on his ego (because, after all, she's got a big one too), loves his aloofness (because it keeps him from owning her) and is intrigued by his belief that life is exactly what you make it. He has high expectations, and so does she. He breaks the rules purposefully and consciously; she does so without realizing there were any to be broken in the first place.

Their only problem arises when the Fire woman decides to fall headlong in love with this perfectly glorious Wood man. She must understand that he loves the world, not just her, and that his friends and social life are more important than any love affair. The Fire woman is capable of acknowledging most of his agenda but could find it frustrating to accept that she's no more special than anyone else. She must accept that he fears intimate relationships, avoids commitment and makes no promises. If she can do all that, then they may have the chance of a successful, albeit unusually liberal and unconventional, relationship.

Sexually, she may find his coldness begins to warm under the sheets. He may not be the most open and passionate man in company, but he is inventive in bed. The Wood man has crafted the art of love-making and will adore the Fire woman's impulse to swing into sexual action at a moment's notice. Neither are concerned with emotional scenes and prefer to live life and enjoy the moment, although it may be the Fire woman who secretly wonders what the next moment or even – dare she think it – the next day will bring.

Fire man/Wood woman

Frankness and honesty are probably the qualities that first draw these two together in a comfortable and spirited rapport. As they begin to realize that they share a mutual need for independence and freedom, they may relax a little closer, confident that neither will suddenly become emotional. However, the Fire man is impatient and often sexually motivated at first – all that friendship business can come after! In contrast, the Wood woman prefers to find a partner she can respect as a companion and good friend first and then as a lover.

For all her prevarications, the Wood woman seeks out the unconventional, and this man may well keep her fascinated for longer than she ever anticipated with his exciting and experimental sexual demands. But Fire is actually quite old-fashioned when it comes to the amorous adventures in love and may insist on taking the lead, choosing the occasion, the environment and dictating the pace. The Wood woman, on the other hand, prefers an informal arrangement, where any conformity is avoided.

The Wood woman defies the norm, and if the Fire man starts to dominate, expecting her to behave in a certain way, she may instantly rebel. However well they respond to one another sexually or mentally, Wood is an idealist, and may still believe that her perfect partner is waiting just around the corner. Fire assumes he is perfect, and looks only inward to his own self; whereas Wood woman has trouble deciding what perfection really means anyway and looks outward to the whole world for answers.

This fundamental difference means that Fire can lose his patience very quickly if Wood's procrastinations continue for too long. While Fire wants results now, Wood needs time to think about what the consequences might be. If they can learn to compromise – Fire to remember the world does exist outside himself, and Wood to accept that intellectual pleasure isn't necessarily the only one to be had in life – then they could share a positive relationship, based on freedom, trust and optimism.

Earth woman/Earth man

These partners have a natural empathy for one another. Their commitment to sensuality is something they may both discover quite soon after their first meeting. However, it may then take them an awfully long time even to get close. Reserved and cautious, Earth doesn't like to chase after anyone, preferring others to come to them. This could mean this courtship may take longer to develop than most other relationships. But then neither will mind: the quality and calmness of the pace is more suited to them both than any dash to get under the sheets.

Earth people need to feel secure and nurtured with a partner before they even consider a more regular commitment. The problem is that once they do feel bound, they can also become emotional, possessive and incredibly jealous.

To an outsider, the erotic nature of this partnership may seem overwhelmingly intense. But for two Earth-dominated people there is little room for doubt in their minds, or their bodies, that physical blending and mutual sensuality are paramount. Their initial communication may be sparse, punctuated by many attempts at self-righteous defences from both until the other begins to drop their mask and relax. Earth people are capable of establishing any liaison they choose and become genuinely committed when they are sure of their feelings for each other. Both are highly in tune with each other's needs, and sexually they may discover instant gratification. Grounding their love-making into a purposeful experience, because they know what's best for themselves, they know what's best for their partner too!

Self-centred sulks may arise occasionally when they choose not to communicate, for both are stubborn about admitting they are in the wrong. Together, they may be equally possessive about money. Most Earth partnerships are sensible. They save, build houses, work for progress and material wealth. However, if the Earth woman is enchanted by a beautiful but expensive work of art, she may provoke the habit-bound Earth man into an angry assertion that they should never spend their money at all.

Love is a sticky word for two Earth partners. It doesn't necessarily mean sex, but when they are having sex they are usually making love. The desire to be inventive, spontaneous or risky just isn't part of their sexual make-up, and so they often hold back from one another, preferring to enjoy the known and not being tempted to try out anything new. Change is unacceptable in the Earth partnership, which is why it is often the most stable and long-lasting of relationships.

Earth woman/Metal man

This is a highly volatile and erotic relationship, as long as the Earth woman is ready for a deeply moving experience. She is the most sensual of all the elements and can seduce the Metal man without much difficulty. For these two, instant sexual attraction is common. The chemistry displays a powerful urgency with no boundaries, where love and hate are often merged into one highly sexual relationship. Metal people have a reputation for being highly sexed and magnetic, but only because they take sex and their own integrity so seriously. Love and sex are part of life's mystery, and the Metal man is always fascinated by an enigmatic woman. The Earth woman may have to realize that if she gives herself to this man it will involve nothing less than her whole self. An offering that may well secretly please her.

This relationship works well if the Earth woman is prepared to express her own sensual and often highly emotional needs. However, the Metal man may not want to share in her deeper feelings, yet he will be intuitively aware of her needs. His desire is to penetrate her mind and soul, which she may well find unnerving at times. The Earth woman has a temper, and this can be fuelled by a Metal man more quickly than any other element. They may fight to the bed or fight until she leaves. But she usually comes back. Her own determination is as powerful as his, and together they can make a formidable couple in any partnership, business enterprise, friendship or marriage, as well as simply lovers. If the Metal man could take the trouble to look into his own heart at his true motives and vulnerability (as he does with such curiosity of his Earth woman), then he may find that she holds the key to his happiness. The Metal man needs someone who aligns themselves with his desire for success, glamour and distinction. The Earth woman may well prefer this kind of partnership to those of a more erratic and unpredictable type.

The Earth woman must feel secure, and the Metal man will offer her financial stability and loyalty. Their biggest challenge is that the Earth woman is a sentimentalist, something the Metal man is decidedly not. Although she may display true affection and warmth, and demand it back, the Metal man would prefer not to reveal anything close to his heart. His curfew on feeling may mean that her usual tenderness becomes more distant, even though the Metal man possesses great sexual magnetism and charisma. If the Metal man recognizes Earth woman's needs, this relationship can offer mutual commitment and friendship, together with the security they both seek.

Earth man/Metal woman

The highly ambitious Metal woman is just as zealous when it comes to her relationships. She may ride to the top in any profession, but she is also fanatical about finding the perfect partner and soul-mate to share the pinnacle of her lonely mountain. On first meeting, the Earth man may seem to carry all the necessary documents to ensure a successful venture to her particular peak.

The Metal woman is shrewd and just as patient as the Earth man. It may take a while for her all-or-nothing energy to emerge, but when it does, the Earth man won't know what's hit him. At first overpowered by her glamour, wisdom and magnetic sexuality, in true Earth style he may become highly jealous if she so much as speaks to anyone else. The Metal woman is not a flirt, but she likes to shine in a crowd. Once they get past the first awkward meetings, however, for they both find it difficult to communicate openly, they may discover they have similar motives in love, sex and life generally.

However, the Earth male is without doubt more interested in the pleasures of the flesh than the Metal woman. While for her, sex is the profound expression of commitment and the meaning of life, for Earth, it is as necessary and as pleasurable as his favourite food. Sensuality is what makes the Earth man high, but for the Metal woman, sex means power and other serious aspects of life. Status and prestige, love and honour walk hand in hand. She needs to be valued and to value what is close to her, as long as it doesn't get too near to her vulnerable heart.

For the Metal woman, Earth is an excellent stabilizer, and they are both practical and self-sufficient. If they decide to form a permanent relationship, the Metal woman will insist on being in control. The Earth man may quite enjoy this, because secretly he likes being manacled to the ground! Although lacking sentimental attachments, underneath her rather cool exterior she has a gentle refuge for the often noisy complaints of the stubborn Earth male. Her astute silence may turn him into a most considerate and no-nonsense lover and partner, someone who can support her on her road to success.

Earth woman/Water man

When these two first meet it is likely that the Water man has been lured by the sensuality of this deeply seductive woman. And to begin with the Earth woman will warm quickly to the ever-changing expressions and conversation of this highly intuitive man.

Water is a romantic who has neither the time nor the inclination to think about or plan the future. However, the Earth woman may already, in her head at least, have committed herself to Friday nights with this man, as they laugh and chatter across the restaurant table.

Earth loves to give, and this woman will be attentive, gentle, kind and nurturing in the hope of something in return. But Water likes to live near the edge; commitment and attending to the demands of others make him feel claustrophobic. The Water man may find the tenacious feelers of the Earth woman's need for immediate responses too much to handle. For her part, the Earth woman may feel threatened as she watches him with her friends, his flirtatious laughter and witty words apparently overriding their relationship. Far from trying to make her jealous, Water simply needs to have a highly social and communicative lifestyle. He is not after sexual adventures particularly, but the Earth woman may well see it as such. The Water man creates his own timetable and friendships, and if the Earth woman tries to make him stick to hers, he may make a hasty escape. The Earth woman needs to be truly loved with passionate guarantees, something that Water is not able to do.

The one characteristic they do share is guts. The

Earth woman may have the strength to put up with such an indifferent and transient man in her life, and he may have the power to change shape enough times to please her. Eventually, however, she may become too possessive for him. It is the core of this woman's nature to possess, but it is also in Water's more elusive nature to avoid that word altogether.

Earth man/Water woman

Earth men often fall in love with Water women faster than any other element, simply because they pose so many inexplicable riddles. The main problem between these two arises from their dissimilar attitudes to life. The Water woman requires constant change, surprises, fun and excitement. She needs to communicate, to persuade and to beguile. What matters for her is to flow through life and entertain herself in the process. She is also acutely alert to the needs of others, always ready to listen and offer advice. Soaking up the energy of every person in the room, she can be all things and all people to everyone she meets. She acts like a mirror to her friends, and yet she rarely gives away much of who she truly is herself.

For the Earth man this is both a challenge and an impossible feather to catch. Earth is drawn to Water simply because she is so elusive, clever and witty. He may swoop down and carry her off in a cloud of romance for a while, but once she feels the chains of ownership close around her feet, she will break free as fast as she can. The Earth man wants his partner to adore him in body, mind and spirit – but especially his body. The Water woman isn't particularly a sensualist.

Yes, she loves sex, but she likes the games, the words and the romance rather than the earthy reality, and she certainly won't be devoted to his body. Her only devotion will be to changing it! Any mention of permanence may send her running, for Water chooses not to commit herself to rootedness, no matter how much she may need to learn that she has roots, too.

Earth woman/Wood man

The Earth woman may withdraw deeply into herself when she first catches a glimpse of the aloof sophistication of the Wood man. The likelihood of these two ever getting together in the first place is small, but they may find an extraordinarily magnetic attraction of opposite natures. Wood wants freedom and informality, while Earth prefers commitment and conventionality. He may find it goes completely against his nature to enjoy a relationship with such an earthy and sensual female. Wood may have great trouble dealing with the responsive Earth woman who has just offered to cook him dinner at his place one night. This man puts a great distance between himself and any possible romantic involvement, and these two are equally far apart in terms of their physical needs and personal values. She is Earth: tactile, pleasure-seeking, emotional, needing to be nurtured and to nurture with sensuality and safe boundaries. He is the unconventional Wood friend, who would really rather study your bookshelves, examine your background, analyse your every motive then maybe fall into bed or love. In contrast to the Earth woman, the Wood man requires little physical contact. Intimacy for Wood means a group discussion or a day's seminar, not the deeply affectionate embrace of the Earth woman. Some Wood men have been known to develop an instant allergic reaction to a woman's cat, flat or deodorant just to avoid getting involved any further in a relationship. Wood wants to live alone with a million friends and a million plans, rather than take on any woman who draws boundaries around their friendship by defining it as US, or MY boyfriend/partner/lover! A lonely Wood man is far happier than a restricted one.

The Earth woman needs a companion who shares her love of one-to-one intimacy, and this man may have profound difficulty in providing her with that joy. If they do fall in love it may be short-lived but extremely physical. Their long-term prospects will rely on Earth's tolerance and devotion in the face of Wood's anarchic relationship needs.

Earth man/Wood woman

The Wood woman seeks to reform, to perfect and yet at the same time maintain her freedom. When she first meets an Earth-dominated man, she may immediately find she defends herself from the self-righteous attitude of this deeply seductive man. Holding strong opinions herself, however, the Wood woman will remain unruffled, aloof and coolly poised. This gives her the time to assimilate everything about him, and usually she has the courtesy and diplomacy to extract herself quickly before the relationship becomes too sticky. Coming across such a stubborn male, she may want to change his routine, his patterns of behaviour and his habitual lifestyle. But she won't have much success. If these two do get along, it will be because they find the challenge of reconciling such conflicting viewpoints irresistible.

Although the Earth man is not exactly spurred into action by any challenge, he may consider that he knows what's best for this highly detached and self-controlled woman, waiting for as long as he can before he finally gets close to her. This usually occurs in a group discussion or at work – in a relaxed and informal atmosphere where the Wood woman thrives. Not for her the intimacy of romantic liaisons, unless they are based on genuine friendship first. The main problem for the Earth male is that although the Wood woman will admire his straightforward and direct approach to life, she won't be too fond of his possessive and conventionally presumptuous side.

The Wood woman could have an easy-going relationship with him if she is prepared to clear up the mess after their many pig-headed rows. Both are stubborn, but in different ways. Convinced that he is right, Earth man refuses to budge on any issue, and the Wood woman will compartmentalize everything, refusing to accept anyone else's opinions simply for the sake of being awkward and different! Wood people know they are unconventional and play on the fact. For the Earth man and his sense of consistency in love as well as in social relationships, this could present the hardest test. The Wood woman may prefer to visit her friends, male and female, whenever she chooses. Open and articulate, she needs a big friendship with the world, not a close encounter of the Earth kind, however much they might amuse one another for a while.

Sexually, Wood prefers physical experimentation

combined with intellectual stimulation. She is terrified of getting too close emotionally, even though her seductive skills are as playful as his. Even though Earth wants to give and receive, Wood won't reveal her feelings to anyone, let alone herself. Despite these many conflicts, this couple will stubbornly refuse to let go of their mutual battle, just for the hell of it!

Metal woman/Metal man

This could prove to be a highly electrifying and erotic relationship. As with any other similar elemental pairing, these two have built-in antennae for understanding the expression and hidden feelings of the other. Metal is the element that energizes intensity and determination. When these two powerful people meet they may well first hate one another, knowing exactly the kind of torrid motivations that are lurking within the other. Yet at the same time they will have a highly magnetic attraction for one another and intuitively sense the deeper pain and vulnerability hiding behind their glamorous appearance.

Both are equivocal, yet both desperately want to discover the mystery of the other. The sexual chemistry between them may be so powerful that they won't have time for riddles or digging up one another's darker side, but all the time they'll be on guard, watching and waiting for the sword to strike. Their relationship may be a contest of egos, often fired off by their compulsive lovemaking and carried through every action they endure together. As a force to be reckoned with, they may impress friends, irritate strangers and generally be the quiet silent types at the party – successful and provocative.

But they have problems with their own need for independence and an insatiable thirst for power. Resentment and vindictive and manipulative behaviour can result if neither is prepared to be more flexible. Because of their secrecy and fear of intimacy, pain and melancholy can flourish in their lonely hearts. The Metal woman is less likely to hide her true feelings than the Metal man, but she can be highly critical and judgemental, leaving him feeling betrayed and impotent, his least favourite emotions. This is a serious relationship, heavy with repressed emotion but strong and powerful because of its provocative nature. Together, loners can make a powerful twosome, especially if joint ventures and a potentially successful enterprise are on the agenda. Then they may enjoy the power games. But both are capable of destroying the relationship with one flash of a steely blade if the going gets too dangerous. Then, it's time to hone their glamorous swords for another killing.

Metal woman/Water man

The usual antics of a Water man don't include the blistering emotional scenes and fiercely driven actions of the Metal woman. She may well benefit from the imagination and compliance of the Water man's mind, but he might find her intolerance drives him away before they even have a chance to properly connect. Communication is high on the Water man's list of priorities. He is acutely aware of the moods and atmosphere around him and will often flow along with other people's choices and habits rather than following his own. The Metal woman, however, may recognize the changes in mood around her, but she won't allow them to distract her from her own agenda.

When they first meet, the Metal woman will be entranced by this light-hearted and unpredictable man who dances in and out of her life. She will enjoy his gregarious nature, his ability to amuse and socialize, his need to entertain and to be entertained. His boredom threshold is low, and she may try to entice him with glamorous ambitions and productive plans that mostly concern her own future. To him, she will seem absorbed in her own world, secretive, melancholic at times and desperately independent.

The Water man may regard this as charming, for it means he can maintain his own free-ranging attitude, and not be pinned down to any plans for next weekend or even dinner that night. The Water man will bring to the surface her deep sexual intensity. But diving to the bottom of the ocean for sexual pearls is not for him. Preferring to live nearer the surface, he is a merman, who needs to breathe the air, rather than a deep-sea diver.

Their main problem is that when he begins to get to know the Metal woman a little better and listens to her heart-rending memories through the night, although he will be sensitive to her hidden fragility, he may begin to glimpse her intensely serious quest for power. For the capricious yet self-effacing Water man, this female may be just too hot to handle.

Water could learn much from her integrity, but he won't play power games. She, on the other hand, may grow tired of his excuses, his non-commital attitude to their relationship and his careless attempts at deceiving her. Far from any desire to wound, it is precisely because he doesn't want to hurt her that he may tell a few white lies: like how he must go and visit his mother this weekend when in fact he's gone on a pub crawl with the crowd he used to know at his last job. If the Metal woman's astute powers of observation are alert, she'll want all or nothing from this man. He may have to choose between a life of frivolity or a woman of power. But for Water there is no black and white in life; there is only another rainbow.

Metal man/Water woman

This could be an extreme and volatile relationship. The Water woman may on first acquaintance hate his chauvinistic attitudes, and be unable to tolerate his unreserved arrogance, even though she may secretly admire it. Her own need to expose the truth won't go down too well with him either, and they may enjoy teasing one another to begin with, certain that each can outwit the other.

The Metal man will find her totally beguiling and be amused by her enchanting and scattered mind. How different from his own penetrating and invasive intellect! The main problem may arise when the Metal man decides that he can teach this woman the art of serious sexual passion.

Although the Water woman loves sex, she doesn't view it as the total fulfilment of life itself. Neither does she like to be taught anything. To learn and discover via her own amusement is fine, but to be controlled by a Metal man with an ambition to reform her is an altogether frightening matter! Change is the most necessary thing in her life, and she won't take easily to a concentration of sexual activity as the be all and end all of existence. She could well test the Metal man's limits, for he demands not only loyalty but adherence to his rules, and he may find he cannot cope when she wants to socialize and he doesn't. Although the Metal man may love glamour and the highlife, essentially he is a loner.

The Metal man likes to unravel mysteries, and the Water woman will certainly present him with one. The mental agility and capricious whims of this woman's lifestyle will amuse the Metal man, but he won't want her constant chatter in bed when he could be moving the earth for her. The Water woman may love his strength, his support and his sexual charisma, but she won't want to drop her friends for him, nor will she put up with the jealous and destructive side of his personality. Water woman may be able to uncover lonely Metal man's true heart, but only if they can both learn to listen to each other's very different secrets.

Metal woman/Wood man

The strong-willed, solitary nature of the Metal woman's outer personality is an instant hit with the Wood man. His broad-minded acceptance of all kinds of people means that someone as charismatic and glamorous as she will present an instant fascination. However much the Metal woman tries to keep her cool, she will be intrigued by the extrovert games the Wood man plays. He seems sophisticated, eloquent and totally co-operative, and his poise and his rather aloof manner can hold her spellbound. Surely this man is just as independent as she is, and if so perhaps they can form a friendship based on loyalty and trust? But the Metal woman's presumptions are soon likely to antagonize the Wood man. Maintaining this rather obscure idealism about relationships, he rarely lets any near to him. If he becomes committed to just one other person, there is always a slim chance that there might be someone better round the corner!

Wood is frightened of being caught out, both intellectually and emotionally, and the powerful controlling nature of the Metal woman may set a few alarm bells ringing. Although they are both self-assured, she is interested only in self for self, while he is concerned with self for the rest of mankind. His grandiose interests and big group-consciousness may arouse her intellectual acumen for a while, until she remembers that his friendship includes everyone, not just one woman.

If the Wood man is scrupulous and wise, he'll know that behind her glamorous mask and ambitious heart there lies a fragile soul. He will have analysed and judged her long before they climb into bed. This may be her downfall, for the Metal woman is only too aware of her need for passion, intense sexual involvement and the transformative experience that can accompany such desire.

If they do find that friendship alone isn't enough for them, he will have to remember that she wants physical passion as well as the eccentric passions of his thoughts. Any pairing of opposite elements can make for electrifying sex. In this case they must remember that the Metal woman seeks deep eroticism, while the Wood man craves detached and intellectual love-making.

Metal man/Wood woman

The Wood woman is confident that she can keep her freedom intact, because she knows the Metal man is just as arrogant and self-possessed as she.

As soon as they meet they may be instantly attracted by their worldly views on love and life. The Wood woman may employ subtle methods to dig deeply, winkling out all the Metal man's intentions. Then she'll check him out for signs of wear and tear from ex-partners or lovers. The Wood woman admires perfection and success in a man, so if he hasn't achieved anything in his life yet, or he's been battered and bruised by relationships, then she is unlikely to be interested. Genuine honesty is what turns her on, as well as experimenting with new ideas and planning her own future. She probably won't include the Metal man in any forthcoming commitment, but he may be included in her phone book along with the rest of her best friends.

The Metal man will instantly respect this woman's detachment, her magical, seductive ways and her unpossessive expression of her attraction to him. Metal likes cool women as well as those he might seek to control. It's almost as if the wilder, unconventional woman who would not normally turn him on is in fact the very one who will have that effect! Theirs could be an on-and-off relationship, particularly for the Wood woman if the Metal man becomes too loaded with expectations about her.

They are both loners in different ways. Wood woman may have a wide social circle, be the most group-conscious and gregarious of women, but she rarely enjoys close one-to-one relationships. Wood women often live better alone than with a partner, but this man may be profound and dedicated enough to his own causes for them to create some kind of partnership that she will see as unconventional. The irony is that the Metal man is a conformist, but will often go out of his way, and in fact out of his mind, to form a relationship with this compelling and independent adversary.

Water woman/Water man

These two have an extraordinary capacity for understanding exactly what the other is feeling, and sometimes even thinking.

When they first meet, their intuition will be heightened. The Water male may feel more comfortable with this woman than any other. His natural inclination is to be caught up in the flow of whatever energy is around him, and a Water woman follows the same rivers and waterways as his own. They are both romantics and will enjoy getting tangled up in each other's fantasies and similar visions.

First drawn together by their mutual quest for beauty and truth, both are gullible in the face of a pretty face or a physical ideal, often believing only in what they see rather than looking deeper to find the soul behind the mask. To protect their own inner nature, Water people wear many masks, including the frivolous, fun-loving charmer, the self-sacrificing martyr, the victim or the saviour. They will become whichever role takes their fancy, seeing it as another turning on the road to experiencing life. Together, these two Water souls may find they can at least understand the many changing faces and games that the other plays.

Versatility ensures that their love-making will involve everything from passion and wild spontaneity, to airy mental mind games. Both prefer to keep their emotions well and truly hidden, enjoying the moment for what it is, not daring to make promises about tomorrow, let alone next week. The sadness is that neither will let the other cross their firmly defined emotional boundaries. They may eagerly absorb everyone else's problems, but rarely attend to their own. This is why, once in love, they will give away very little of themselves.

They both have a fear of loneliness and prefer to live in a partnership or with friends, but they also have a need for variety, change and exploration. If they can allow the other to travel freely, then they may resolve this problem. Both have the imagination and perception to give one another the space they so badly need for their individuality to take shape.

Water woman/Wood man

These two will dance together without tripping over one another's feet.

When they first encounter one another, the Water woman will be amused by the Wood man's strange way of approaching. Cool, courteous and ambivalent about his motivations towards her, he will find her impossibly elusive, both mentally and physically. However, the further he has to delve, the more he'll enjoy the intellectual challenge, for Wood men thrive on stimulating and unprejudiced conversation rather than dogmatic opinions – he has enough of his own to worry about!

Neither of them desires conventional commitment. The Wood man has a need for a rather oblique loneliness and independence. He must have close friends, and many of them, but within his circle, no matter how big or small, he will remain detached and free-spirited. The Water woman will adore being part of his eccentric world, spending many hours listening to his friends' problems, sympathizing with their feelings and generally employing her mind. He will be highly amused, attracted to her spontaneous and unpredictable gestures and her ephemeral attitude to life, which may also include him. At times she may take him too lightly, refusing to support the more rigid viewpoints which he likes to impose on all around him! She may also be frustrated by his dedication to everyone else's emancipation apart from his own. This sets up a challenge for her, and a Water woman, for all her unfocused qualities, needs a big wall to climb. Her restless nature feeds off dissension, as long as it's not of her own making.

Sexually, they blend well together. Emotion and deep sensuality are not fundamental to their bedroom antics. Some nights they may prefer to talk under the full moon about the universe, or set their deckchairs up on the lawn at midnight and simply watch the stars. It is here that Wood man may learn from the Water woman's wisdom. And one night he may be lucky enough to find himself enlightened enough to acknowledge his own inner feelings.

Water man/Wood woman

The inquisitive Water man may find a great deal of genuine, though not emotionally obvious, sympathy from the seductive and unbiased Wood woman. When they meet (probably at some work event or party, for both are social animals), the Wood woman will want to analyse and dissect this bright, breezy and witty man. He may talk non-stop about everything under the sun, but he won't give much away about himself. This is likely to instantly magnetize the Wood woman's intellectual acumen as well as a few heartstrings. For what is this man really about? They both have the same easy attitude to life, although at times the Wood woman can be stubborn and opinionated just for the sake of it, and the Water man inconsistent, fickle and very unreliable. But the Water man will always want to communicate with the Wood woman, simply because her scatty manner keeps him on his toes. She may have problems keeping up with his restlessness and indiscriminate plans and ideas. His mood changes may fascinate her, for they seem to reflect everyone around them rather than his own true intentions. The Wood woman needs a friend first and a lover second, and this man could prove to be the closest she'll get to maintaining her freedom, yet knowing someone cares.

Together they could confront the fear of failure which they both have about their sexuality. Wood's fear of intimacy won't be threatened in the laid-back arms of the Water man, and equally he can drift along, confident that she won't aim an emotional spotlight at his face. His intuition means he is always prepared for any unusual twists and turns in their relationship. For the Water man instinctively knows when the Wood woman needs to move forward, either in her career or socially, and will be happy to follow in her wake. Their only problem will be if he becomes over-sensitive to her need for perfection, and she begins to wonder if he can live up to her ideal.

Wood woman/Wood man

If both parties are equally happy to follow their own lives, and can genuinely allow their partner the freedom that they both so desperately seek, then this blend of non-possessive harmony could last a lifetime. Being the same element, they have a natural affinity for reform, for perfection and for the good of the whole. Their universal compassion will be forcefully noted and felt by others, and their sense of rightness and social equality shared with enthusiasm and intellectual debate. However, because both are so busy pursuing their humanitarian goals, they don't have an awful lot of time to share between the sheets.

What attracts them in the first place is their mutual ideal of a romance that lasts for ever. However, the monotony of constant physical closeness or the day-to-day routines of living together may spoil this deep inner need for romantic pleasure. Theirs is a relationship that may work better if they live separately. Alternatively, they could be separated by work or social necessity, so that they enjoy each other's company again when they re-group at home.

Wood people require sophisticated love. It must be fashioned and refined, cultivated to produce more than just sexual encounters or mental stimulation.

Almost bordering on the spiritual, it must be as awesome as the universal landscape they both visualize.

The only problem they may have is in expressing their needs, for they both fear to reveal too much of their deeper selves. But together they can draw up an unstated agreement, an intuitive understanding that whatever the other does or says, it's OK to be like that. If both partners are self-aware, then their tolerance and acceptance of the other will improve. The Wood man is more likely to be judgemental when riled, but by seeing his reflection held like a mirror before him in the form of his Wood partner, he'll start to bend a little in his views. Although sensitivity to others is not high on their list, sharing the experience of being human is, providing they can do it separately, merging only when the moment is right for both.

Talking is probably their greatest passion, and it is through conversation that their greatest union will be found, even though they still may refuse to discuss their deepest fears or feelings. Sexually, they can create the ideal environment, the romantic and perfect physical experience, and yet they will always seek more than simply human love. Perhaps together they may find it.

Chapter Ten
The Elemental Family

This final chapter provides an insight into how each birth or key element functions within the family unit. It will allow you to discover how parents deal with their children and vice versa. Remember, if you are in a different phase of elemental energy than your birth element, use the Fivefold Year rituals and enhancements to balance you.

Fire

At home you are determined to be the leader. You need to make decisions quickly, and if your family fails to live up to your time schedules, you'll be impatient and demanding. You need action and excitement, and are passionate about your home and the people who share it with you.

The Fire parent

Fire parents are dynamic and full of optimism for the future. They expect their children to be just as excited by anything new, for they are much like children themselves. Fire parents understand the difficulties of growing up, but lose patience if their offspring become stubborn, obstinate or bad-tempered, which, of course, children often do!

The Fire mother is particularly prone to pushing her children to go out and have fun, take riding lessons and enjoy unusual sports, in the hope she can inspire them. The Fire father may not be interested in his children's eventual careers, but he'll certainly want them to win all the prizes at school. Fire is very competitive, and Fire parents will be high-achievers for their children.

Fire parents have difficulty with Metal children, and this combination works well only if the Metal child is given responsibility and a set of rules to work by. Although fire isn't awfully fond of rules and regulations, the Fire parent might find life less rigid if they allow their Metal children to show their determination or dedication to a cause. Battles of wills may ensue, and often it is the Metal child who is more wilful and stubborn than its Fire parent. Fire would rather just move on to the next event than hang around for the showdown.

Fire parents do well with Wood and Earth children, providing them with plenty of opportunities to learn how to look after themselves and assert their needs. Alternatively, these children may reward their Fire parents by widening Fire's vision to embrace more than their own self-centred world. Wood and Earth children relax with Fire around and just let the Fire parents get on with it!

Fire parents find the Water child the most complex of all. But there is a strong bond between them, precisely because they are so very different. The Fire parent may shriek with irritation when the Water child becomes restless and bored, hiding in the bathroom for an hour, then suddenly eating everything in the fridge. Fire will never come to terms with the ebb and flow of their Water children, but Water will be highly tuned in, and almost psychic, about their parents' moods and daily dramas. Water children quickly learn how to stick up for themselves, and at some point the insensitive Fire parent might begin to realize, much to their delight, just how entertaining, witty and funny their Water child can be.

Fire people do make excellent parents, especially for extrovert and highly sociable children, as their energetic, pioneering approach is highly infectious. However, a Fire mother or father can be too pushy, expecting too much from their children. Later in life their children might feel they have to live up to lofty ideals that can never be achieved.

The Fire child

Fire children are full of boundless energy and can be a handful when small. They require some kind of routine to give them a sense of organization and conscience. Too much discipline, however, will drive them into reverse gear, so that they refuse to do anything. Fire children feel uncomfortable unless all their needs are met *now*, and if they can't get what they want they often rebel or become wild and irascible at school.

The Fire child's high energy levels are better engaged through playing games and sports than sitting still in the classroom or helping out their parents. Fire offspring need something to get their teeth into. If their energy can be channelled into their passion, they are less likely to suffer from outbursts of temper or angry and impatient moodiness. With careful handling, a Fire child will be able to use their competitive spirit to the full, providing they don't decide to run the household themselves first!

Home style

Fire people need a stylish interior in their homes. They may prefer brash colours and wild lighting, dramatic paintings or outrageously abstract fabrics. If you're Fire, make sure you have one room or an area that is devoted to *you*.

If rampant colour schemes don't give you a thrill, then incorporate reds and oranges in your curtains, upholstery or even on the edges of pictures and mirrors. Hang mirrors that reflect the sunlight, and use rubber plants, cacti or bells, fantasy posters and firework scenes in your decor. For a Fire child, paint silver stars on the ceiling, wild animal pictures or bonfire scenes on their walls. Hang a crystal in the south-facing window to assert your fiery needs.

Earth

At home you are sensible, creative and affectionate, enjoying the company of a serene family life. You love nature and need to make sure your routines are maintained, and that family and friends are nurtured and loved. You are almost managerial in the way you take responsibility for the family, and your home must be filled with beautiful objects or sentimental treasures that remind you of the past.

The Earth parent

Reliable and dependable, the Earth parent can easily instil a sense of purpose and consistency into their children's lives. However, Earth parents always know what's best for their children, sometimes to the exclusion of anyone else's ideas.

The Earth parent wants to maintain a quiet and fairly routine environment, and Mother Earth will be exactly that: nurturing, supportive and highly capable. Exuding emotional caution, she is perhaps too watchful when her children want to play outside, and over-anxious when they bring their teenage friends around to sit upon her antique sofas. Earth parents are not very adaptable, and may find it difficult to accept that their children have as much right to make choices as adults. Yet Earth people will guide their children through the art of logical decision-making and the need for forethought.

An Earth parent builds for the future. They need to take a managerial role in the household and ensure that everyone gets their fair share. Earth fathers may tend towards dogmatism and conservative attitudes. They fear change, and won't enjoy the rebellion of youngsters with precocious ideas! Investment in the future and financial security are essential for a happy Earth parent. If they feel their children are getting the best, whether in their education or simply their environment and status, then the Earth parent is quietly satisfied. But they will want to see the results of their efforts. Earth parents can be too rigid and old-fashioned, and the Earth mother's over-protective, and tenacious side can cause difficulty when the children grow up and want to leave home.

The Earth parent may find Water and Wood children difficult to handle. Both require flexibility of mind and the freedom to do as they please. They may not live up to the traditional standards of the Earth parent, as both are liberal and fairly unconventional. The Metal child, on the other hand, could have a much more stimulating relationship with its Earth mother, as both share the need for stability and enterprise. The Fire child could enliven the Earth parent with their high energy levels. Earth parents tend to see the serious side of life too much, and a Fire child could bring humour and fun into the family environment, providing Earth has the patience (which they usually do) to handle the tantrums and the self-centred moodiness.

The Earth child

Earth children are strong-willed and very affectionate, but they are usually determined to do things their way. They can be extraordinarily creative and artistic if given the chance, and prefer to pursue indoor activities or easy-going sports that don't require much team effort. They love food and their possessions, and trouble can arise if they are not taught to share at an early age. Earth children can get very clingy towards their parents, and their toys.

As they grow older they may refuse to let their friends share their food, borrow their clothes, make-up or music. They also become quite jealous if their closest chums make friends with someone else, for the Earth child's loyalty is unquestionable.

Although they may insist that they are always right, their ability to care for and support their siblings or friends makes them popular. At school the Earth child may respond well to the disciplines and boundaries imposed on them. More than anything the Earth child needs a stable and comfortable territory from which to venture out into the world; then he may go far. Without this stable and peaceful environment, he may become rigid and lazy, greedy and demanding at an older age. Although the Earth child may seem to plod when others charge or race, he always gets there in the end. As they mature, Earth children become rational and sensible about life and their relationships, and feel happiest within the confines of convention.

Home style

The Earth home must be warm and filled with beautiful objects, paintings or natural colours and textures. Earth people respond well to collections of stones or pebbles, bowls of rock crystal and antiques. If you're an Earth person, make sure you include terracottas, ochres and dusky desert yellows in your colour scheme. Bring loofahs, sponges, shells and rocks into your bathroom, and keep your kitchen filled with old jars and spices. The luxuries of life are important in the Earth environment, so bathe in sensual oils, use old fabrics, paisleys and tapestries in your decor or as curtains. Japanese landscapes will improve your vitality if hung in the bedroom. Invest in a bonsai tree, as Earth is probably the only element who has the patience to tend it! Children may enjoy richer colour schemes in their rooms. Include coffees and greens, rich umbers and images of wildlife, the jungle or nature.

Metal

At home you verge on the minimal in all you say or do. You prefer peace and tranquillity to wild parties or never-ending family quarrels and feuds. You may prefer to live alone, but if you are a family member you will almost certainly want to be in charge. You command respect, and you also insist on routines. Your family members must have a certain amount of self-confidence, commitment and integrity, and be prepared to put up with your extremes when you can be either the funniest person on earth or the most depressed!

The Metal parent

The Metal parent is both a wonderful instigator of new ideas for their children, and a superb role model for enjoying life to the full. The drawback is that they desperately want their children to succeed, and this can get out of all proportion. The Metal parent, albeit quite unconsciously, can be too strict at the toddler stage, preventing the child from discovering the world for itself. The Metal parent has strong principles, and may not allow the child as much freedom in their choices of clothes, sport or friends as perhaps they would like. But the Metal parent can also encourage and direct their offspring in shrewd and often intuitive ways. Keeping them occupied and busy with school work, games and new skills is easy for the Metal parent. Taking charge and motivating their aspirations in life is no problem. What they do find difficult, however, is to moderate their critical side and their need to stick to the rules. This lack of tolerance can extend to their children.

Metal parents are good role models for successful and highly individualistic people. They are good in a crisis when their children are taken ill, or come home from school complaining about their teachers or friends. The Metal father or mother's career may, however, take precedence over their role as a parent, and this can cause conflicts within the family. The Metal mother is not fond of domesticity and although she has great love for her offspring, may not be very demonstrative or affectionate towards them.

The Metal parent relates well to Water and Earth children. Water babies are so very different from their mothers and bring a lightness and humour into their parents' lives. Water children can adapt easily to the territorial aspect of their Metal parents, knowing that it won't be too long before they can leave home and enjoy a grown-up friendship with them. Earth is not terribly flexible and will enjoy the guidance and boundaries imposed on them. Fire may fight with a Metal parent, and Wood will certainly rebel as a teenager, if not before!

The Metal child

Metal children have many strings to their bows and by the time they are old enough to walk have usually analysed their family and know exactly how to get what they want from them. Being kept active and busy is essential if Metal children are to develop purpose and meaning in everything they do. Otherwise they are likely to undermine their siblings or friends, and manipulate their parents into giving them everything they want, when they want it. Metal children are powerful, and their highly resilient appearance hides a seriously emotional intensity inside, which needs to be channelled through sports, creative work or music. The Metal child must be doing, otherwise they may resort to undoing!

Metal children can be more jealous than the other elements of the arrival of a new baby in the household. Their fear of rejection is intense, so the parents would be well advised to talk this through, perhaps encouraging the Metal child to help with the baby. Excellent at school, Metal children thrive on their own success, and as they mature will enjoy the challenge of anything from athletics, horse-riding and the martial arts, to political debating. Most Metal children enjoy reading, and may take an interest in history, archaeology or in solitary sports like mountaineering or swimming.

Home style

Metal people are unconcerned about frivolous decoration or too many possessions. They thrive best in an environment where gold, silver and images of wealth are prominent. Kitchens are excellent places for Metal to display stainless-steel utensils, fine etchings or line drawings against white walls. Use gilt-framed mirrors in your hall or sitting-room, and metal bedsteads in your bedroom, to enhance your integrity and self-esteem. For power and success you may need to place a 'money-tree' (any of those succulents with leaves shaped like coins, which can be found in most garden centres) in the corner of your bathroom, or hang silver and gold threads or chains from the end of your bedpost. For children, use gold stars on their walls and doors, paint their rooms with vibrant light colours and incorporate gold-coloured fabrics in their bedlinen.

Water

At home you are the great communicator. Always chatting to your family, or on the phone to your friends, you enjoy lively and stimulating company. Your children must be your friends, and partners should take equal responsibility for their upbringing. You may be flexible towards your family's needs, but you'll need to escape as often as you can to recharge your sensitive and imaginative nature.

The Water parent

The Water parent's greatest difficulty will be to impose any kind of structure or discipline on their children's daily life. Water hates to be told what to do, and likewise will resist correcting or scolding their children for anything. Water parents, however, have the magical ability to understand whatever it is their child wants, needs, feels or thinks. Whether psychic or attuned, the Water mother in particular, will be responsive to her young toddlers, and find endless joy in playing their games, amusing their minds, as well as getting them out and about. The more the Water parent can find to do with their children, the better for both. Water parents are children at heart, and restless with it. They may spoil their children more than other parents, but their genuine flexibility and imagination mean their children will be happy, spirited and as gregarious as they are.

The Water parent's wide-ranging experiences and interests will stimulate and awaken much knowledge in the younger child, but they may face the problem of bending the rules too often, and being unable to make decisions. The older child and teenager may find their Water mother unbearably restless and changeable, and perhaps too charming and pleasant with everyone she meets or knows. Water parents often rely too strongly on the child's ability to make their own decisions, rather than offering solid guidance.

Water parents do best with Water, Wood and Fire children. They may prefer the company of adults to the intense conflict with a Metal offspring, even though they'll try desperately to understand the drive behind this child's behaviour. With Earth they may become frustrated at the rituals and routines the child prefers, but, adaptable as ever, Water will at least listen and try to learn. The Water parents' weakness is that they can make too many sacrifices for their children, neurotically running to and fro on their behalf, then interfering in their relationships and friendships later in life.

The Water child

This is a child of great sensitivity and awareness of others. They may grow up as any other child, but will prefer to live in the world of their imagination for as long as possible. Life is an awfully hard place for the Water child, and to escape into dreamland or fantasy play, books and artistic pursuits will help alleviate the pressure of knowing what the whole world is thinking all the time! The Water child must be stimulated mentally and will enjoy playing as many games and learning as many skills as possible. Boredom is the biggest problem, and because they are so eager to start a new game or activity, finishing anything may prove an impossible task.

The Water child hates being told what to do and will be clever enough, as they mature, to find many ways to elude parents, teachers and friends. But the Water child remains helpful and adaptable, willing and giving as long as others understand their need for spontaneity. At school they enjoy witty conversation and active or practical subjects, but may drift into a dream world in the more academic lessons. Often attracting a wide circle of friends, Water may want to socialize more and more as they grow into their teens. Teenage Water girls may be fickle and unpredictable, but they'll always be popular; Water boys may need to focus themselves on recreational activities that channel their quicksilver energy.

Home style

The Water person is happiest in an environment that offers change and fascination. True to Water's nature, fast-growing plants, darting fish and running water – a fountain, or paintings and scenes of wrecks, ships, fierce seas and waterfalls – will stimulate and bring harmony to their home. If you're a Water person, you may find your life is enriched by incorporating stones and rocks from the sea in your bathroom decor. As for colours, use violets, Prussian blues and inky hues in a favourite room of the house. Incorporate a fish tank, or stone cups filled with coloured water, blue candles and light music in your bedroom. Place amber or aquamarine crystals on the window-ledge of a north-facing room for inspiration and peace.

Wood

If you're a Wood person, although your home won't be a status symbol, it will certainly exude an eccentric and unconventional quality. You'll need space, unclut-tered rooms and someone else to do the domestic work if you can! Your family needs to stimulate your mind, and you'll probably be pretty liberal about their own views, freedom and motivations in life. As long as no one attempts to order you about or take advantage of your good nature, you'll be happy to share in family life. However, your freedom is something you'll not give up gladly.

The Wood parent

Avoiding conflict comes naturally to the Wood parent. As soon as they sense the possible onset of tantrums, battles or irritable teenagers, they'll coolly change the atmosphere or channel the child's energy in a positive way. Wood can make tremendous parents if, and only if, they can remain slightly detached from any emotional contact. If their offspring are in need of affection, they will certainly show it, but it won't be bear hugs and kisses; it's more likely to be displayed by warm words and kind expressions.

Wood parents, especially mothers, are economy conscious, and they'll expect the same care with money, possessions and people from their children. Wood parents have unusual standards, which will offer much younger children opportunities to experiment with anything from hi-tech games to building a tree-house in the wild garden!

The Wood parent has a natural talent for organization, and so may prove a strong and supportive model for their developing offspring. Wood fathers are willing to discuss any subject under the sun, and may well know all about it as well! They make superb teachers, and can offer diplomatic and broad-minded advice to their older children. However, children can see this open approach to life as an easy ticket to do as they please, and Wood parents may experience more rebelliousness from their teenagers than they had anticipated.

Wood parents may shudder at the demands made on them when their children are babies. This is not an easy age for the Wood parent, but if they can get through these first few years, they will find that their children become their friends, something they truly treasure. Wood parents get on well with the charming Water and the inspirational Fire children. They may battle with Metal offspring and find that Earth children become fretful and whining if subjected to a home that has no obvious discipline.

The Wood child

The Wood child is sociable and unpossessive with his friends and toys. Often a popular but unconventional soul at school, they work erratically but with a sharp and inventive mind. Other children may find the Wood child charming, but a little self-centred and aloof, a reflection of their innate need to be detached from intimacy. They'll have many acquaintances and enjoy the company of their siblings and family, but they will need plenty of space.

The Wood child can be encouraged to do well at school, as long as they are not overtly disciplined. They may excel in the arts, for they have a strong aesthetic sense and musical ability. Anything different will amuse them, and they may choose strange or unlikely friends as they mature. The Wood toddler is renowned for being bossy, but they will become more cooperative once they reach school age and realize they are not the only child in the world! The Wood child thrives on an informal and yet fairly controlled environment. They need routine, but they also need to deviate from it as well. Breakfast may always be at seven-thirty, but the choice on offer must be varied. Jam on toast one morning, eggs the next, or perhaps let's try jam on eggs for once!

Home style

Wood people need a sophisticated and unconventional home where they can feel grounded. They may prefer unusual buildings, converted warehouses or old rambling houses and apartments, as long as they have the space and scope to make it as near their ideal as possible. If you're a Wood person, you may spend more time out of your home than in it, but to enhance and harmonize all aspects of your lifestyle, incorporate some Wood elements. Obviously, your furniture, books and plants are natural Wood enhancements, so use these to their advantage. Books are wonderful for establishing your ambitions, so keep a pile of your favourite volumes in the kitchen or bedroom. Use colours like mint green, olive green, soft twilight hues and natural tints. Make your staircase into a feature by adding spreading plants or gnarled wooden sculptures at the top and bottom. Otherwise, bring in paintings or posters that contain some visual reference to steps or ladders, or place a piece of green tourmaline or malachite on an east-facing window-ledge to connect you to progressive vision.

Last Words

By following your current energy wisdom of Fire, Earth, Metal, Water or Wood, you are also discovering more about *you*.

Becoming more aware of who you are in relation to the world and the environment, and understanding that partners, friends and family may have a very different energy resonance to your own, means you are beginning to weave the five Elements into your life. This is only a beginning, but it represents the first step on the journey to harmonious living.

The ancient Feng Shui masters were often artists, poets, philosophers and scholars, but they were also just ordinary people who wanted to ensure balance and harmony in the natural world as well as in their own lives.

When you use Feng Shui for yourself, remember also to use it for the good of mankind, of all living things, and particularly the planet Earth that is 'home' to us all.

The night was peppered with stars . . . they were crowding round the house, as if curious to see what was to take place there.

from *Peter Pan*, by J. M. Barrie